Based on the Netflix
series *Waffles + Mochi*,
created by Erika Thormahlen
and Jeremy Konner,
featuring Michelle Obama

NETFLIX

Learn to Cook
Tomato Candy, Gratitouille,
and Other Tasty Recipes

WAFFLES + MOCHI™

GET COOKING!

RECIPES BY
YEWANDE KOMOLAFE

FOREWORD BY
MICHELLE OBAMA

PHOTOGRAPHS BY
KELLY MARSHALL

CONTENTS

FOREWORD

by Michelle Obama

Hi there!

I'm so excited to introduce you to my friends, Waffles and Mochi! These two best buds just love to eat, and their passion for food has taken them on adventures all around the world. From California to Italy, from Japan to Peru, they've met with some of the best chefs on the planet to learn about how flavors and ingredients and spices shape the meals we eat every day.

So many of the foods we see everywhere—tomatoes, potatoes, corn, rice—have a story to tell. Where do they come from? Are there different varieties? And why are they so delicious?

That's what this cookbook is all about: answering those questions . . . and enjoying some great food!

Over the next hundred pages, you'll explore all the parts of a good meal—saltiness and umaminess and sweetness and so much more. You'll learn new ways to make dishes with items you can grab at your local grocery or corner store! And you'll even get tips from expert chefs like Samin Nosrat and José Andrés who Waffles and Mochi met on their adventures!

What you'll find is that no one has to travel as far as Waffles and Mochi did to eat scrumptious meals. You don't even have to be a professional chef—we can all make these meals right at home!

Some of my favorites are Chef Samin's Tomato Candy Pasta (page 12), Gazpacho Party by Chef José (page 20), Tortellini Soup by Chef Massimo Bottura (page 74), and Chef Preeti Mistry's Pani Puri Party (page 84)! Don't forget about Second Chance Cookies (page 36) as a yummy dessert!

Even if you've never baked, sautéed, or chopped vegetables before, you'll discover that cooking can be fun and easy—and that sharing your creations with family and friends afterward is the greatest part. Because at the end of the day, when you make something with love, it's going to be good.

So are you ready for an amazing adventure? Let's get cooking!

Love,
Mrs. Obama

INTRODUCTION

Before we get started, we have a confession to make—of the culinary kind!

(Taking a deep breath.)

WE ARE NOT CHEFS! And yet, here we are, introducing a cookbook! After a foreword from Michelle Obama (aka "Mrs. O")! AHHH!

(Calming down.)

Okay. How did we get here?

Well, just like our favorite ingredient explorers, Waffles and Mochi, we are *huge* fans of food. But we are even bigger admirers of the talented chefs and cooks who make mind-blowing magic in the kitchen when they make mouthwatering meals. Because that's what cooking is to us: a superpower. Like flying over buildings or becoming invisible, when a chef turns water into a tasty soup, or flour and eggs into tortellini, it's pure wizardry. And yet we believe with a little practice—and a big, adventurous spirit—everyone can be a food superhero. Hey, it's called a *super*market, after all!

That's why we're so excited Waffles and Mochi met up with Brooklyn-based, Nigerian-born chef and writer Yewande Komolafe, whose superpower lies in crafting unfussy recipes with palate-popping flavors. The three worked together to translate recipes from the show using the ten ingredients Waffles and Mochi tackled on their Magicart missions for Mrs. O.

None of the recipes are too complicated or require too many tools, and they are for a range of skills so everyone in the family can help—from expertly boiling an egg to whizzing up gazpacho in the blender to roasting mushrooms for the ultimate umami flavor.

All of our friends from the store are here to cheer you along the way, including shopping and cooking tips from Busy Bee, Steve the Mop, Shelfie, and Intercommy, too! Plus, you'll meet your taste buds and learn recipes that'll make those best buds sing.

Remember: If a puppet can cook, so can you.

Are you ready to get cooking?

Jeremy Konner &
Erika Thormahlen

Creators and showrunners
of *Waffles + Mochi*

COOK LIKE A PRO!

My name is Yewande and I'm a *New York Times* food columnist and cookbook writer.

I created the recipes in this book! I grew up in the city of Lagos, Nigeria, and all throughout my childhood our backyard garden produced herbs, vegetables, and fresh fruit year-round. I learned from a very young age that cooking is the experience of transforming fresh ingredients into exciting, unforgettable meals. I am thrilled to be sharing these recipes with you.

Even though I attended culinary school after college and spent years working in restaurants, bakeries, and test kitchens, these recipes are designed for anyone and everyone. Yes, there are some recipes in this book from some of the world's most creative chefs, but they've been adapted and tested to work in your home kitchen—with tools you might already have.

Whether you've been cooking and baking for years or you are just starting your culinary adventure, these recipes will allow you to explore the ingredients, techniques, and—most important!—flavors that make cooking fun.

Cooking is an adventure! It's fun when you're curious, courageous, and, most of all, . . . prepared. There are a few things to do before you start cooking that should clear the way for a successful expedition.

DRESS THE PART WITH:

- an apron, to keep your body and clothes clean
- oven mitts, to protect your hands from the heat

READ THE RECIPE—from start to finish. The recipe is like a map to your destination. You'll want to know where you're headed before you begin.

GATHER YOUR TOOLS. Now that you've read the recipe, you know what kinds of tools you'll need. Take them out and place them nearby. Here are some common tools you'll need for this book:

- measuring spoons and cups
- tasting spoons
- scissors for snipping herbs
- tongs
- small, medium, and large bowls
- baking sheet
- saucepan
- parchment paper
- whisk
- spatula
- blender
- strainer
- stand mixer or handheld mixer

PUT EVERYTHING IN PLACE. The recipe's ingredient list tells you how much of each ingredient you need and sometimes whether it should be chopped, peeled, or grated. Ask an adult for help with knives. Many things can be cut up with scissors, too! Chefs like to have their ingredients prepared and set out so they can see them before they start cooking. This is called *mise en place*, which is French for "put in place."

PLATE LIKE YOU MEAN IT. Many people say that we eat with our eyes first—that means we want our food to taste good *and* look good. Be creative when you place your food on plates to serve. Think about where each color goes, how the shapes look together, and how the sauce is drizzled. There are no rules about what it has to look like. Just make it look good to you!

TOMATO

MAKES 2½ cups

TIME: 50 minutes

simple squeezed tomato sauce

1 (28-ounce) can peeled **whole tomatoes**

¼ cup **olive oil**, plus 2 tablespoons for drizzling

4 **garlic cloves**, smashed and peeled

1 teaspoon **coarse salt**, plus more to taste

HAVE YOU EVER seen a juicy red tomato and thought, *I just want to squish it to bits!*

Well, now is your chance. This simple recipe channels your hands' squishing power into a yummy, garlicky sauce you can spread on pizza or serve over cooked pasta.

Only every time I mop the produce section!

1. Pour the tomatoes into a medium bowl. Use clean hands to squeeze them to release the juices and break them down into smaller pieces (or use the back of a wooden spoon).

2. In a medium saucepan, heat ¼ cup of the oil over medium heat. When the oil is shimmering hot, add the garlic and use a wooden spoon to stir frequently, cooking the garlic until fragrant and softened, about 2 minutes.

3. Add the tomatoes and stir. Bring the sauce to a simmer, then reduce the heat to medium-low and cook, stirring occasionally until it deepens in color and reduces to about two-thirds of its original volume, about 40 minutes.

4. Sprinkle in the salt and the remaining 2 tablespoons oil. Stir and remove the pot from the heat. Taste and adjust the seasoning with additional salt if necessary. Allow the sauce to cool slightly before using.

5. To store, let the sauce cool completely and transfer to a storage container with a lid. Refrigerate for up to 3 days or freeze for up to 1 month.

MAKES 1¾ cups

TIME: 5½ hours (mostly inactive!)

samin's tomato candy pasta

2 pints **cherry tomatoes**, stemmed

¼ cup **extra-virgin olive oil**

½ teaspoon **sugar**

Fine sea salt

1 pound **short pasta**, such as penne

1 cup freshly grated **parmesan cheese**, plus more for serving

16 **fresh basil leaves**

HAVE YOU EVER had tomato candy? Our friend Samin Nosrat, who is a chef and cookbook author, created this extra-special recipe for Waffles and Mochi that uses tiny, sweet tomatoes called cherry tomatoes. It's a delicious treat and a healthy reminder that the best things come to those who wait. Slow-roasting tomatoes really brings out their sweetness and makes them taste like fruit—which is exactly what they are!

And the texture might be the real star here! As the skins crisp up, the interior becomes chewy and the flavors burst with each bite, just like candy.

1. Position an oven rack in the center of the oven and preheat to 225°F. Line a baking sheet with parchment paper.

2. In a large bowl, toss the tomatoes with 2 tablespoons oil to coat. Add the sugar and ½ teaspoon salt and gently toss again to coat. Using your hands, but being very careful not to squish the tomatoes, spread them out on the lined baking sheet.

3. Transfer them to the oven to bake. Every 30 minutes or so (between binge sessions of your favorite show!), check on the tomatoes and jiggle the pan to make sure they are not sticking, and rotate the pan 180 degrees (front to back) to keep the tomatoes cooking evenly.

(RECIPE CONTINUES)

BEE FLEXIBLE!

* If you don't have time to slow-roast the tomatoes, increase the oven temperature to 350°F. Skip the sugar (it will burn at the higher temperature) and toss the tomatoes with only the olive oil and salt. Roast as directed until the tomatoes are shriveled and just starting to split, about 45 minutes. Tomatoes cooked at this temperature won't be quite as sweet, but they will still be delicious!

✱ Tomato candy is so delicious that you'll want to double—or even triple—this recipe, especially in the summer when tomatoes are in season. Store extra tomato candy in a glass jar, cover the tomatoes with olive oil, and refrigerate for up to 6 weeks. Or freeze them in a single layer on a baking sheet until solid and then pack them into freezer bags and freeze for up to 6 months.

Bake until the tomatoes are semi-dried and shriveled and start to taste like candy, about 5 hours. Remove from the oven and keep warm.

4. When the tomato candy is almost done, bring a large pot of water to a boil over high heat. Add enough salt to make the water taste really salty—like the sea! (Aim for about 1 heaping tablespoon salt to 7 quarts water.)

5. Add the pasta, stir, and cook until it is just under al dente—try saying it aloud, "al dan tay"—which means the pasta is still firm when you bite into it, about 1 minute less than the package directions. Use a cup to scoop out 1 cup of the pasta cooking water (you'll learn why in the next step) and set aside. Drain the pasta and transfer it to a large bowl.

6. Add the tomato candy, parmesan, and remaining 2 tablespoons olive oil to the bowl of pasta. Tear the basil leaves into the pasta in large pieces or use scissors and get to snipping. Stir everything together. Now here's a chef's secret: Sometimes the pasta needs a little more moisture to help everything come together. If you find that your pasta is a little dry, add 1 to 2 tablespoons of the extra pasta cooking water to help the cheese and basil cling to the pasta.

7. Taste your dish and add more salt if you think it needs it. Serve hot with more parmesan!

Howdy, chefs! I'm Tex—that's short for Texture. I'm a taste bud that works for your tongue, but I don't care about how things taste. I'm here to see how food *feels*.

That's right. You know all about taste and smell, right? But our tongues *touch* our food, too. Is it dry as the desert or gloopy like glue? That's texture!

Here's a rip-roaring adventure you and your tongue can go on together. Find foods with many different textures in your pantry and give 'em a whirl!

The texture of our food can affect our mood—the more we chomp down on crunchy foods, the happier we are!

Taste It!

- Chomp on a crispy food.
- Chew on a chewy food.
- Which one took longer to chew?

Texture changes how food sounds, too! A loud crunch or a squishy squeak could make all the difference in a dish.

Taste It!

- Try something soft.
- Try something crunchy.
- How did they *feel*?

Cooking food changes its texture. Think about a delicious carrot. When it's fresh, it's crunchy. When it's cooked, it's soft.

Taste It!

- Try a smooth food.
- Try a lumpy food.
- Which texture did you like better?

SERVES 4

TIME: 20 minutes

tenacious tomato salad

¼ cup **neutral oil**, such as canola or grapeseed

1 tablespoon **Yaji Salt** (page 30)

1 tablespoon **roasted peanut oil**

2 cups **torn bread pieces**

3 ripe **tomatoes**, any variety, quartered or cut into wedges if large

2 large **plums** or other **stone fruit**, pitted and quartered

Coarse salt and freshly ground black pepper

1 tablespoon **honey**

Grated **zest and juice of 1 lime**

4 ounces **goat cheese**

1 cup **mixed fresh herbs**, such as dill, mint, and basil

HERE'S SOMETHING WAFFLES and Mochi were surprised to learn: Tomatoes are hard to define. You might think they're a vegetable, and in 1883 the U.S. Supreme Court ruled that they legally are a vegetable. But, actually, they're a fruit! At least botanically and scientifically speaking. If you cut into one, you'll see that it's bursting with juices and seeds hiding beneath its skin. But chefs and home cooks treat them as vegetables because of their ability to transform from bright and slightly sweet to rich and downright salty.

So the tomato is a vegetable—and it's also a juicy fruit! The fact that the tomato never gave up on finding where it belongs makes it the hardest-working ingredient at the table. It may have started out as a berry on a bush in Peru, but then it went on to take over the world, even though it's still not widely known as a fruit. That's tenacity!

This salad celebrates the tomato's fruity side by pairing fresh tomatoes with tart, sweet plums. There are more than 10,000 varieties of tomatoes—big, small, round, oblong, striped, red, purple, yellow—so use any variety that is at its freshest and ripest.

1. In a large shallow saucepan, heat the neutral oil over medium heat until it shimmers, about 1 minute. Remove from the heat and add the seasoning salt and peanut oil. Swirl to combine.

2. Transfer 2 tablespoons of the spiced oil to a small bowl. To the oil remaining in the pan, add the torn bread pieces. Set the pan over medium heat and toast the bread, stirring frequently, until browned and crispy, 8 minutes. Remove from the heat and set aside.

3. In a large bowl, gently toss the tomatoes and plums with 1 teaspoon salt and a pinch of pepper. Allow to marinate for at least 5 minutes.

(RECIPE CONTINUES)

4. To the bowl with the reserved 2 tablespoons spiced oil, add the honey, lime zest, lime juice, and a pinch of salt and whisk to combine.

5. To assemble the salad, use a tablespoon to scoop portions of the goat cheese into the bowl of tomatoes. Add the toasted bread and the dill, mint, and basil leaves. Drizzle in the dressing and fold gently to combine. Transfer the salad to a platter or individual plates to serve.

Don't define me so fast. I'm here to say at last, baby, I'm a fruuuuit!

WHERE DO TOMATOES BELONG?

Cold refrigerator air makes the tomato's texture mealy and unappealing, so store your fresh tomatoes at room temperature so they taste their best. You can ripen firm tomatoes by placing them in a brown paper bag and letting them soften on your counter for 3 to 5 days. Firm tomatoes can be used in cooking and are best for preserving or cooking Simple Squeezed Tomato Sauce (page 11).

SHELFIE'S GUIDE TO

GROCERY SHOPPING

No one knows the shelves of the supermarket better than a talking shelf—that's me!

I'm Shelfie, and the supermarket is my home. I think you'll like it here. It's full of delicious foods, ingredients, and things people need to cook. If you want to be an expert grocery shopper, try some of my favorite tips, from my market to yours.

1. Before you shop, make a list! The supermarket has so many things in it, you might forget which items you need! Write or draw the items on a piece of paper.

2. Find fresh foods (fruits, vegetables, herbs, baked goods, meats, eggs, milk, and cheese) on the outside aisles. Fresh foods taste best soon after you buy them.

3. Look for anything that comes in a box, can, bottle, or bag on the inside aisles. Foods in these aisles are typically shelf stable and will last longer in your cupboard. This is also where you'll find cleaning supplies, cooking tools, and food for your pet.

4. Swing by the Land of Frozen Food for some of the freshest food in the store. Look for bags of frozen fruit and veggies, which are flash frozen at peak ripeness and stored in big freezers. That way, they stay nice and cold and last longer than fresh produce! It's also where you'll find ice cream—and our friends Waffles and Mochi!

5. If you can't find something you need, ask someone! Grocery store staff know the aisles almost as well as I do. The aisles will be numbered, starting with Aisle 1—so look up above at the signs!

6. Bring your own bags so you can reduce waste! Lightweight bags are great for holding produce, but any bag will do—even your backpack!

SERVES 4

TIME: 20 minutes, plus 1 hour chilling time

gazpacho party

4 large **tomatoes** (about 1 pound), coarsely chopped

½ **green bell pepper**, seeded and chopped

1 **seedless cucumber**, peeled and chopped

1 **garlic clove**, chopped

2 tablespoons **sherry vinegar**, plus more to taste

2 teaspoons **salt**, plus more to taste

¾ cup **extra-virgin olive oil**, plus more for drizzling

Crusty bread, warmed and sliced for serving

EVER CRAVE A bowl of soup on a hot day? Well, you might if it were served cold! Our friend José Andrés, one of the most famous chefs in the world, serves gazpacho, which is a chilled soup he learned to make from his wife. Originally associated with the Andalusian region of southern Spain, gazpacho can be made anywhere because the ingredients—tomato, cucumber, green peppers, and bread—are found everywhere. That's what Chef Andrés loves so much about this soup: It belongs everywhere!

This recipe uses your blender as a cooking tool. Time to shake things up and get the party started! What ends up in your bowl is creamy (from the olive oil), tangy (from the sherry vinegar), and fresh (from the veggies you toss in).

1. In a large bowl, combine the tomatoes, green pepper, cucumber, garlic, vinegar, and salt and allow to stand for 10 minutes at room temperature.

2. Transfer the tomato mixture and its juices to a blender. Puree on high until completely smooth. With the motor running, slowly stream in the olive oil and puree until the mixture is emulsified. Taste and adjust the seasoning with additional salt and vinegar if necessary.

3. Transfer the mixture to a large bowl and chill for at least an hour or until cold.

4. To serve, stir and ladle the cold gazpacho into bowls (see Shhh . . . Here's a Cheffy Secret). Top with a drizzle of olive oil. Serve with slices of warm crusty bread for dipping.

Shhh . . . Here's a Cheffy Secret

To plate this just like Chef Andrés, dice extra tomatoes, cucumbers, and peppers and arrange them in each bowl before you pour in the gazpacho.

SALT

SERVES 4

TIME: 45 minutes (plus time to make the mole)

chicken mole enchiladas

1 tablespoon **neutral oil** (such as canola or grapeseed)

Coarse salt

1 pound **boneless, skinless chicken thighs** or **breasts**

12 **corn tortillas**

1½ cups **mole**, homemade (see page 26) or store-bought

4 ounces grated **Cotija cheese**

½ cup **Mexican crema**

¼ cup chopped **fresh cilantro**

THIS RECIPE CALLS for ready-made sauce, whether it's from a family recipe or your favorite jarred variety. Or use the mole you made from the recipe on page 26. As you assemble the ingredients, you can sazón or season with salt to taste—by adding just a pinch at a time.

Make this recipe meatless by substituting the chicken with Umami's Favorite Mushrooms (page 97) and skip steps 2 and 3.

1. Preheat the oven to 350°F. Lightly grease a 9 × 13-inch baking dish.

2. Fill a small pot halfway with water and bring to a boil over medium heat. Reduce the heat to a simmer and season the water with salt. Add the chicken and poach until cooked through and tender, about 15 minutes.

Poaching is like boiling, but the bubbles in the simmering liquid are much slower. Watch out because the water is just as hot!

3. Move the chicken to a large bowl and when cool enough to handle, shred it using your fingers or a fork.

4. In a small skillet or nonstick pan, warm up the tortillas one at a time until softened. Stack the tortillas on a plate lined with a kitchen towel and cover them to keep warm while you finish the recipe.

(RECIPE CONTINUES)

5. Assemble the enchiladas: Fill each tortilla with 2 to 3 tablespoons of the shredded chicken and 1 tablespoon of the mole. Roll up the filled tortilla to form a cylinder, then place it seam-side down in the prepared baking dish. Arrange the tortillas tightly next to one another in the dish.

6. Spoon ¼ cup mole over the top of the tortillas and sprinkle them with half of the Cotija. Cover the baking dish tightly with foil.

7. Bake the enchiladas until heated through, about 25 minutes. Remove the foil for the last 5 minutes in the oven.

8. Serve the enchiladas hot, topped with the remaining ½ cup mole and 2 ounces Cotija. Dollop with the crema and sprinkle with the cilantro.

MAKES 1½ quarts

TIME: 1 hour 30 minutes

mole sauce

TO LEARN MORE about how salt adds flavor to our food, Waffles and Mochi visited the Queen of Flavor in Los Angeles, California! Bricia Lopez is a Mexican-American chef and cookbook author who is from Oaxaca, Mexico, which is also the birthplace of mole, a sweet and smoky sauce made with salt and chocolate. She knows how to make the ultimate mole!

This mole recipe is meant to be one path on the way to all of the mole you'll hopefully taste in your life. There are many variations of this sauce, and there is no one right way to make it. But any version has something no other food has—a deep, almost emotional feeling that connects us to the earth and the ingredients it shares with us. The spices, fruits, seeds, and vegetables we love are all part of its remarkable journey to the delicious reward waiting for us at the end!

8 large **guajillo chiles**, tops trimmed and seeded

2 pounds **Roma (plum) tomatoes**

1 large **yellow onion**, quartered

6 **garlic cloves**, peeled

2 tablespoons **dried oregano** leaves

2 tablespoons **dried thyme** leaves

1 teaspoon **whole cloves**

1 teaspoon **allspice berries**

¼ cup **white sesame seeds**

½ cup **raw almonds**

½ cup dark or golden **raisins**, soaked in hot water to plump, then drained

¼ cup **coarse fresh bread crumbs**

¼ cup **neutral oil**, such as canola or grapeseed

2 **cinnamon sticks**

4 ounces **Mexican chocolate** or **unsweetened chocolate**, chopped

Fine sea salt

1. Preheat the broiler to high.

2. In a heatproof medium bowl, place the dried chiles and pour enough hot water over them so they're submerged. Set a small bowl on top of the chiles to keep them submerged so they can rehydrate, about 10 minutes.

3. Arrange the tomatoes, onion, and garlic on a sheet pan. Broil, turning occasionally until they are browned all over, about 20 minutes. Remove from the oven and set aside.

(RECIPE CONTINUES)

4. In a large dry skillet, combine the oregano, thyme, cloves, allspice, and sesame seeds. Toast everything over medium heat, stirring frequently, until the spices and sesame seeds are warmed and smell really good, 2 to 3 minutes. Transfer the mixture to a mortar and grind it up with a pestle or use a spice grinder.

5. Drain the chiles and transfer to a food processor or blender. Working in batches if you need to, add the charred vegetables, along with any juices that may have collected in the pan. Puree the mixture until smooth, while you do the blender dance. Add the toasted spices and sesame seeds, almonds, drained raisins, and bread crumbs. Puree everything until smooth.

I always watch for splatters!

6. In a large soup pot or Dutch oven, heat the oil over medium heat until shimmering. Slowly and carefully pour in the pureed mixture so it doesn't splatter. Stir the mixture, add the cinnamon sticks, and allow the sauce to come to a simmer, about 5 minutes. Cook, stirring frequently, until the sauce thickens and is reduced by about one-third, 35 to 40 minutes.

7. Stir in the chocolate and allow the pieces to melt into the sauce. Cook for another 10 minutes. Season with salt just a little at a time, tasting along the way until the flavor is just right. Serve. To save this for later, store in an airtight container in the refrigerator for up to 1 week or in the freezer for up to 1 month. Warm cold mole gently in a pot over low heat.

Chocolate for dinner?!

LEFTOVERS? LUCKY YOU!

Make the mole ahead of time and cool completely. Store in an airtight container in the refrigerator for up to 1 week or in the freezer for up to 1 month. Warm cold mole gently in a pot over low heat. Try using your mole sauce in creamy, saucy Chicken Mole Enchiladas (page 23)!

EACH MAKES ¼ cup

TIME: 5 to 10 minutes

just a pinch of salts

ONE OF THE best ways you can make your taste buds sing is by adding a little salt to your cooking. Sometimes just a pinch of it can make the world of difference in taste! Add a few extra ingredients and you take salt to the next level.

Veggie Lover's Salt

GET EXPERIMENTING WITH dried ingredients you find in the grocery store. Use this salt in soups, over eggs, or in veggie dishes to add a little extra umami.

1 teaspoon **fine sea salt**

1 loose cup **dehydrated vegetables**, such as dried mushrooms, nori sheets, or dried beets, crumbled

1. In a small bowl, combine the salt and dehydrated crumbled vegetables.
2. Working in batches if you need to, use a spice grinder or a tabletop mortar and pestle to grind or crush and incorporate the vegetables and the salt.
3. Transfer the vegetable salt to an airtight container, cover, and store at room temperature.

Yaji Salt

A NORTHERN NIGERIAN spice blend, *yaji* is typically used to season grilled meats. With its blend of warm spices, it also balances the tart flavors.

¼ cup **unsalted dry-roasted peanuts**

1 tablespoon **ground ginger**

2 teaspoons **cayenne pepper**

1 teaspoon **garlic powder**

1 teaspoon **fine sea salt**

1. In a mini food processor, chop the peanuts or work in batches using a spice grinder. Pulse just enough to grind into a coarse powder.
2. Transfer the peanut powder to a small bowl and stir in the ginger, cayenne, garlic powder, and salt.
3. Transfer the seasoning salt to an airtight container, cover, and store at room temperature.

Za'atar

THIS SPICE BLEND is a staple in Middle Eastern cooking and will be the most versatile salt in your pantry, too! It tastes a little like pizza. Sprinkle it over boiled or scrambled eggs, tomato salad, a rice and vegetable bowl, or baked salmon.

2 tablespoons **dried marjoram** or **oregano**

2 teaspoons **ground sumac**

1 teaspoon **dried thyme**

1 teaspoon **fine sea salt**

1 tablespoon **sesame seeds**

1. In a small bowl, combine the marjoram, sumac, thyme, and salt. Working in batches if you need to, use a spice grinder or a tabletop mortar and pestle to grind or crush and incorporate the herbs into the salt.

2. Add the sesame seeds to the bowl and stir to incorporate with the herb seasoning.

3. Transfer the seasoning to an airtight container, cover, and store at room temperature.

Sugar Spiced Salt

SALT ISN'T JUST for savory foods; it also brings out the sweetness (yes, that's right!) in desserts and baked goods. Sprinkle this spiced salt over sugar cookies, a slice of pie, or banana bread.

2 tablespoons **sugar**

1 tablespoon **ground cinnamon**

½ teaspoon **fine sea salt**

¼ teaspoon **grated nutmeg**

Pinch of **ground cloves**, **cardamom**, or **allspice**

1 tablespoon **citrus zest**, such as orange or lemon (optional)

1. In a small bowl, combine the sugar, ground cinnamon, salt, nutmeg, and cloves. Working in batches if you need to, use a spice grinder or a mortar and pestle to grind or crush and incorporate the spices into the sugar and salt mixture.

2. Add the zest (if using) and incorporate with the spiced seasoning.

3. Transfer the seasoned spice to an airtight container, cover, and store at room temperature.

TRY IT!

MEET YOUR TASTE BUDS

I'm Sweet. I love sugar! But I'm not all about desserts. I think every meal could use a little sweetness—even tomato sauce. Some of my favorite foods are bananas, corn bread, and honey!

Taste Sweet!

- Find something in your pantry that's sweet.
- What did you try?
- How did your buds react?

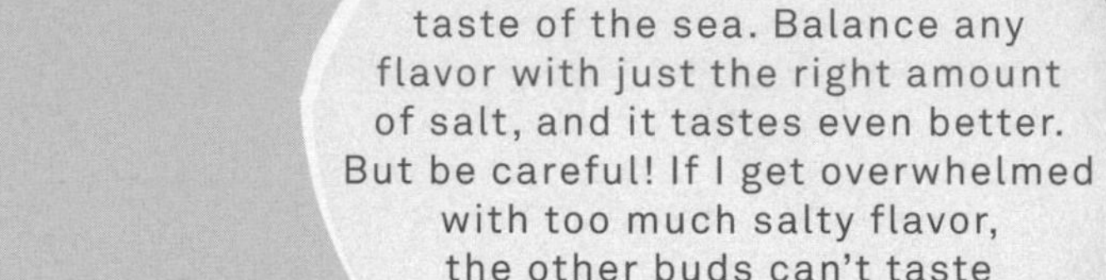

Argh! I'm Salty. I love the taste of the sea. Balance any flavor with just the right amount of salt, and it tastes even better. But be careful! If I get overwhelmed with too much salty flavor, the other buds can't taste their flavors at all.

Taste Salty!

- Find something in your pantry that's salty.
- What did you try?
- How did your buds react?

I'm Sour. If it were up to me, all foods would be an adrenaline rush! You'll find me digging into any food that makes your mouth pucker, like lemon, pickles, or yogurt.

Taste Sour!

- Find something in your pantry that's sour.
- What did you try?
- How did your buds react?

Flavor Fact

Some people think the tongue is like a map, but it's not! The truth is you can taste all the flavors on all parts of your tongue. The only exception is that the back of your tongue has more bitter sensors.

What makes food taste good? Well, our tongues are covered in thousands of tiny little things called taste buds. These buds have sensors that send our brains information about the flavors in our food, and some buds are super focused on a certain type, helping us to tell the difference between them.

Flavor Fact

Flavor isn't all about taste—your sense of smell is a powerful factor. Hundreds of types of sensors in your nose send information to your brain as you eat and help give you a fuller sense of the flavors. Your nose can detect at least a trillion different scents!

My name is Umami. I prefer the finer things in life. You know, when there's a rich, savory taste you love but can't describe? That's me! I can detect certain acids that leave your tongue and brain satisfied! You'll find them in savory foods, like mushrooms, ketchup, and soy sauce.

Taste Umami!

- Find something in your pantry that's savory.
- What did you try?
- How did your buds react?

I'm Bitter! I'm the protector. I keep you from eating anything poisonous by making you spit it out. You're welcome! But bitter isn't bad. My favorite foods you should try include celery, kale, and very dark chocolate.

Taste Bitter!

- Find something in your pantry that's bitter.
- What did you try?
- How did your buds react?

sauces for your taste buds

HAVE YOU EVER tasted something and thought it was a little bland and boring? Maybe your taste buds just needed more flavors to excite them! Here are some sauces to experiment with on different foods. Try them! How do they change the flavor of the food?

SALTY-SWEET SAUCE
(PAGE 99)

SOUR-SALTY SAUCE

TEX'S CHEESY SAUCE

MAKES 1 cup **TIME:** 10 minutes

Sour-Salty Sauce

½ cup **full-fat coconut milk**

2 tablespoons **tamarind concentrate**

1-inch piece **fresh ginger**, grated

1 **garlic clove**, grated

½ teaspoon **ground turmeric**

1 tablespoon **honey**

1 teaspoon **coarse salt**, plus more to taste

½ cup sliced or chopped **fresh herbs**, such as scallions, cilantro, basil, or mint

1. In a small bowl, combine the coconut milk, 1 tablespoon of the tamarind concentrate, the ginger, garlic, turmeric, honey, and salt.

2. Taste and add more salt and another tablespoon of tamarind if it needs it. The tartness of store-bought tamarind concentrate may vary, so start with a tablespoon at a time, adjusting the amount as needed. The sauce should taste tart but not overwhelmingly sour.

3. Stir in ¼ cup of the herbs. Reserve the remaining herbs to garnish the salad. Store in an airtight container in the refrigerator for up to 3 days. Stir before serving.

MAKES 1 cup **TIME:** 5 minutes

Tex's Cheesy Sauce

TEX WOULD LOVE this textural sauce. Spoon it over roasted vegetables or chicken or use as a dressing for salads.

Grated **zest and juice of 1 lemon**

3 tablespoons **vinegar**, such as rice, sherry, or white wine

1 teaspoon **honey**

1 teaspoon **freshly ground black pepper**

¼ cup **olive oil**

½ cup crumbled or grated **salty cheese** such as feta, parmesan, pecorino, or Halloumi

Sea salt (optional)

¼ cup **chopped herbs**, such as dill, parsley, mint, or basil

1. In a medium bowl, combine the lemon zest, lemon juice, vinegar, honey, and pepper. Drizzle in the oil and whisk together until emulsified.

2. Stir in the cheese and taste. Adjust the sauce with some salt (if using). Stir in the chopped herbs. Store in an airtight container in the refrigerator for up to 3 days. Stir before serving.

MAKES 2 dozen cookies

TIME: 45 minutes to 1 hour, plus 4 hours chilling time

second chance cookies

BROWN SUGAR, BUTTER, chocolate, and just a pinch of sea salt—these might be humble ingredients, but throw them together and they create a magical dessert that everyone will want seconds of, including Mrs. Obama!

When Waffles and Mochi made these cookies with Baker, they learned from an important mistake. Baker's recipe called for adding "salt to taste" to finish the cookies. Instead of adding just a little sprinkle, they poured a lot, saddling their taste buds with too much saline. Good thing Baker had another batch! These cookies are a tribute to them—it's always good to have a second chance so you can try again.

- 2¾ cups **all-purpose flour**
- 2 teaspoons **baking powder**
- ¾ teaspoon **baking soda**
- 1 teaspoon **coarse salt**
- 2 sticks (8 ounces) **unsalted butter**, at room temperature
- 1¾ cups packed **dark brown sugar**
- ¼ cup **granulated sugar**
- 2 large **eggs**, at room temperature, lightly beaten
- 1 tablespoon **vanilla extract**
- 2½ cups **semisweet chocolate chips**
- **Flaky sea salt**, for sprinkling

1. In a medium bowl, whisk together the flour, baking powder, baking soda, and coarse salt. Line a baking sheet with parchment paper.

2. In the bowl of a stand mixer fitted with the paddle attachment (or in a medium bowl with a handheld mixer), combine the butter, dark brown sugar, and granulated sugar and beat until light and fluffy, about 3 minutes, scraping down the bowl with a rubber spatula as needed. Add the eggs and vanilla and beat until the ingredients are just combined.

3. Using a rubber spatula or wooden spoon, fold in the flour mixture and chocolate chips until they're just incorporated. Use the mixer to further mix until combined, about 1 minute.

4. Drop heaping tablespoons of dough onto the lined baking sheet using a spoon. Space the scoops close together so all the dough fits. Cover the pan loosely with plastic and refrigerate for at least 4 hours and up to 12 hours.

5. Preheat the oven to 350°F.

6. Remove the cookies from the refrigerator. You can bake up to 8 cookies on a baking sheet. Decide how many you are going to bake now and transfer the rest to a resealable bag to store

Just a pinch of salt! I learned that the hard way.

for later (see Dough Ahead). Leave 2 inches of space between the cookies. Use your palm to flatten the top of each cookie (to help them spread evenly).

7. Bake, rotating the pan front to back halfway through the baking time, until the cookies are golden brown, puffy, and just set in the center, about 14 minutes. Remove the cookies from the oven and tap the pan on the counter to deflate the cookies.

8. Salt the cookies to taste by sprinkling them with a pinch of salt. Transfer to wire racks to cool completely. Repeat to bake more batches of 8 cookies each. The baked cookies will keep in an airtight container for up to 3 days.

Dough Ahead

The cookie dough will keep, covered or in resealable bags, in the refrigerator for up to 1 week.

SERVES 4

TIME: 10 minutes, plus 30 minutes marinating time

salty's roasted fish

4 **fish fillets** of your choice (6 ounces each), skin on or off

1 pound **Swiss chard**, **kale**, or any **hearty leafy greens**

1 cup **Sour-Salty Sauce** (or any of the other sauces on pages 35 and 99)

½ cup sliced **scallions** (or other herb of choice)

4 tablespoons **olive oil**

Coarse salt

Lime wedges, for squeezing

FISH AND SEAFOOD are delicate—they cook quickly and do a marvelous job of allowing other flavors to come through. They also have a natural saltiness from the sea that can be enhanced with marinades. Here, fresh fillets soak up a coconut-tamarind sauce before being tucked into greens and broiled on a sheet pan. The marinade that reduces on the pan can be spooned over the finished dish, and the results are juicy, salty, and—because of the tamarind—a little sour, too.

1. Pat the fish fillets dry with paper towels, then wash your hands. Remove the tough stems of the leafy greens and tear the leaves into 2-inch pieces. Set the greens aside.

2. In a large bowl, combine the sauce with ¼ cup of the scallions and add the fish fillets. Toss to coat the fish pieces in the marinade. Allow the fish to marinate for 15 to 30 minutes.

3. Position a rack in the top slot of the oven and set the oven to high broil.

4. Spread the greens on a sheet pan. Drizzle them with 2 tablespoons of the oil and use your fingers to rub in the oil. Season with salt and toss to coat.

5. Place the fish between the greens, tucking a few pieces under the fish. Spoon the sauce over the fish and drizzle the remaining 2 tablespoons olive oil over the top. Transfer the pan to the oven and broil the fish, rotating once, until the fish is tender and the greens are just beginning to brown, 8 to 10 minutes depending on the thickness of the fillets.

6. Divide the fish and wilted greens among plates and drizzle the pan juices over the fish. Garnish with the remaining ¼ cup scallions. Serve immediately with lime wedges.

POTATO

SERVES 4

TIME: 1 hour and 15 minutes

the anything-but-ordinary baked potato

4 large **baking potatoes**, such as russets

4 teaspoons **neutral oil**, such as canola or grapeseed

Coarse salt

4 tablespoons **unsalted butter**

Freshly ground black pepper

½ cup grated **sharp cheddar cheese**

¼ cup chopped **cooked bacon** (optional)

¼ cup **sour cream**

¼ cup sliced **scallions** or **chives**

DO YOU THINK potatoes are boring? Well, Waffles and Mochi did, too, until they learned how awesome taters are! The potato has been essential to humans throughout history and is used in so many cuisines around the world. It's both nutritious and adaptable, able to be grown in cold and tropical climates alike—it can be grown even in space, and maybe one day on Mars! That's because it already contains all it needs to grow, and it doesn't require a lot of light. What else makes it special? It can taste soft, delicate, and earthy on the inside, and be crunchy and crusty on the outside. See? Potatoes are far from ordinary. They're unique—just like you!

1. Preheat the oven to 400°F.

2. Scrub the potatoes with a vegetable brush or clean sponge under running water. Using a fork, poke holes all over the skin of each potato. Rub each one with 1 teaspoon oil and sprinkle it with salt. Place them in a baking dish or on a baking sheet.

3. Transfer the dish to the oven and roast the potatoes until they are soft and a fork poked into the center goes right through, about 1 hour.

4. Remove the potatoes from the oven and allow them to cool slightly. Cut the potatoes open by slicing each down the middle. Open up the halves and add 1 tablespoon of softened butter to each. Sprinkle each half with some pepper.

5. Divide the cheddar, bacon (if using), sour cream, and scallions among the baked potatoes and serve immediately.

BEE FLEXIBLE!

There's no limit to how to build the perfect baked potato. Close your eyes and think of toppings that will excite all of your taste buds: crunchy, salty, sweet, or slightly acidic. What toppings can you imagine?

TRY IT!

GROW A POTATO FROM A POTATO

Have you ever seen a potato that has waited so long to be cooked that it started to sprout right there in your pantry? That's because potatoes grow from other potatoes—they're kind of like their own seed. Potato farmers save part of their harvest to start next year's crop.

If you have a sprouting potato, you can use it to grow more potatoes of your own. Here's how:

STEP 1: Find a planter, a bucket, or other large container that has drainage and fill it with 4 inches of soil. Place a sprouting potato on the soil, making sure the majority of the "eyes" are facing up. This is where the leaves will sprout. Cover the potato with about 1 inch of soil.

STEP 2: Place the container in an area that gets sun.

STEP 3: Once a plant starts to sprout from the soil, start watering it regularly (about every 4 days, depending on the amount of light your space gets). Keep the soil moist, not soggy.

STEP 4: As your potato plant grows, add more soil to the container. Keep adding soil as your potatoes grow until the container is full, so that only a few leaves are showing.

STEP 5: When the plant starts flowering, that means there are new potatoes under the soil! You can harvest them gently or wait until the plant starts to wilt to dig up bigger potatoes with thicker skins.

STEP 6: Pick out a potato recipe and start cooking! Yum!

Here in the garden, we grow the most wondrous assortment of vegetables, fruits, and herbs. But you don't need to have a whole rooftop to grow your own food. You can start with a sunny window.

Flavor Facts

- Potatoes came originally from South America but over the centuries have become important to cuisines around the world.
- Potatoes were the first vegetable grown in space. Scientists hope to one day grow them on Mars!

SERVES 4 to 6

TIME: 1 hour

herby smashed potatoes

NOW THAT YOU'VE **hopefully tried simple baked potatoes (page 41) with toppings, let's give them a smashing new look. That's right: After boiling small potatoes to soften them, pull them out of the water and let them have a good whack with your hands! Then sear them in a pan, and you've got a crispy-textured morsel perfect for seasoning, salting, and dipping into your favorite condiments.**

Coarse salt

2 pounds **baby potatoes** such as Yukon Gold or red-skinned

¼ cup **neutral oil**, such as canola or grapeseed, plus more as needed

2 to 4 tablespoons **condiments of choice** (see Tasty Tip)

½ cup chopped **fresh herbs**, such as parsley or dill

1. Line a plate with paper towels and set it aside.

2. Bring a large pot of medium salted water to a boil over high heat. Use tongs to carefully add the potatoes. Cook until a fork poked into the center goes right through, about 25 minutes. Drain the potatoes and transfer to a baking sheet until they're cool enough to hold.

3. Using your hand or the flat bottom of a cup or jar, press down gently but firmly on each potato until it smashes but still holds together as one piece.

4. In a skillet, heat the oil over medium heat until it shimmers, about 2 minutes. Working in batches, use tongs to carefully transfer the potatoes to the skillet in a single layer. Cook them without moving until the bottom of each potato is browned and crispy, 4 to 5 minutes. Flip with the tongs and cook the other side until crispy, about 3 minutes.

5. Move them to the plate lined with paper towels. Repeat with additional oil until all the potatoes are cooked.

6. Transfer the warm potatoes to a medium bowl. Add the condiments of choice and gently toss using the tongs to coat them. Sprinkle them with the herbs, transfer to a platter or individual plates, and serve.

Tasty Tip

For condiments, try Better Than Butter (page 79), Tex's Cheesy Sauce (page 35), or 1 teaspoon of one of the seasoning salts (see pages 30 and 31).

SERVES 4

TIME: 1 hour

delicioso stew

3 tablespoons **unsalted butter** or **neutral oil,** such as grapeseed (preferred) or canola

1 medium **yellow onion**, minced

2 **garlic cloves**, minced

2 cups diced peeled **butternut squash**

2 cups diced peeled **white potatoes**, such as russet

Coarse salt

1 tablespoon **ají amarillo** or **ají chili paste** (yellow or orange chile paste; optional)

2 cups fresh or frozen **mixed vegetables**, such as corn, peas, and diced carrots

½ cup **heavy cream**

¾ cup grated **fresh Cojita cheese** or cheddar cheese (about 4 ounces)

¾ cup grated **Gruyère cheese** (about 3 ounces)

PÍA LEÓN, OUR chef friend who lives in Peru, makes this yummy dish in a skillet over an open fire. The flames cook the ingredients quickly and evenly, creating a cheese sauce that coats the potatoes and vegetables. Since we can't always cook outside, this dish is a creamy casserole that's easy to make inside. It has all the elements of Pía's dish, including the fiery finish that happens under the oven's broiler, which is its highest setting.

Cooking with heat takes care and patience. You want to wait for the oven to heat up, but when you pop your dish in the oven, you can't forget about it. So make sure to plan out your steps before you dive in, get your pot holders and apron ready, and be sure to set a timer!

1. Preheat the oven to 400°F.

2. In a large ovenproof skillet, heat the butter over medium-high heat. Toss in the onion and sauté until softened, 4 to 5 minutes. Add the garlic and sauté until it smells fragrant, about 1 minute.

3. Toss in the squash and potatoes and stir until coated with the onion mixture. Season with salt and stir in the chile paste (if using). Add the mixed vegetables and cream and allow everything to come to a simmer. Stir in half of each of the grated cheeses.

4. Transfer the skillet to the oven and bake until the potatoes and squash are tender, about 25 minutes—to check, just poke them with a knife or skewer.

5. Remove the skillet from the oven and turn the broiler to high.

6. Top the potatoes and vegetables with the remaining grated cheeses and broil until the cheese is bubbling and browned in spots, about 8 minutes. Serve hot!

PICKLES

MAGICART'S GUIDE TO

PICKLING

A pickle isn't just something you eat; it's also something you do! People all over the world pickle food. The process involves fermentation, and it keeps food from spoiling while making ingredients taste great. Pickling has been around for centuries, and the science behind it hasn't changed much in all that time. It's all about bacteria.

Some pickles are made by stopping bacteria from growing. Other pickles want *more* bacteria! Here are two types of pickles:

VINEGAR PICKLES: When a food is sealed inside a jar filled with vinegar, the food is protected from bacteria that would normally cause the food to spoil quickly. Bonus: It takes on the delicious flavor of the vinegar and any herbs and spices added to the brine!

FERMENTED PICKLES: When a pickle is fermented, you *want* to let the good bacteria grow. Soaking the food in a salty brine gives the naturally occurring bacteria a chance to transform sugar into a substance that protects it from harmful bacteria. That keeps it from spoiling! Like vinegar, this substance—called lactic acid—tastes sour, which gives the food that classic pickle flavor.

MAKES 2 quarts

TIME: 5 minutes, plus 3 to 7 days curing time

not your typical pickle

A SHARP BITE and a quick snap—a great cucumber pickle is the ultimate rush! What makes it so fun is the sourness that comes from the vinegar, which causes your mouth to pucker, like a fish. These pickles take patience to make, but the good news is you'll end up with two jars: one to keep and another to give to a friend. They'll be tickled to get these pickles!

This recipe is flexible—it allows you to pick your pickles. Sub in your favorite vegetables and any herbs and spices you have on hand and the recipe is guaranteed to work here. Try different things—you'll be surprised. Maybe there's something you don't love raw but you will love fermented!

6 to 10 **dill sprigs**

1 tablespoon **coriander seeds**

1 teaspoon **black peppercorns**

1 pound **mini seedless cucumbers** (7 or 8), trimmed and quartered lengthwise into spears

1¼ cups **apple cider vinegar, distilled white vinegar,** or **rice vinegar**

2 teaspoons **coarse salt**

1. Gather two 1-quart canning jars with lids and rings and clean them with warm soapy water. Rinse well and allow them to dry completely.

2. Divide the dill, coriander seeds, and whole peppercorns evenly between the clean jars. Pack the cucumbers into the jars snugly, making sure they fit tightly in each jar.

3. To make the brine, in a large bowl or a liquid measuring cup, combine the vinegar, salt, and 1½ cups water. Stir until the salt dissolves completely.

4. Once the salt is dissolved, pour the liquid into each jar, completely immersing the vegetables. Cover the jars tightly with the lids.

5. Allow the jars to sit at room temperature while the cucumbers are becoming pickles! This magical transformation should happen within 3 to 7 days. The longer you allow your pickles to sit, the more sour they will become. Leave at room temperature for up to 3 days for crisp, half-sour pickles.

LEFTOVERS? LUCKY YOU!

Jarred pickles will last, unopened, for 6 months. Store in a cool, dry place such as a cupboard or pantry. But once the jar is open, you should move them to the refrigerator, where you can store them for up to 1 month. Use only clean utensils (and never your fingers) to pull pickles out of the jar so you don't contaminate the jar.

MAKES 2 cups

TIME: 10 minutes

WITH THEIR ACIDITY and sweetness, pickles really sparkle in your mouth! But sometimes you just can't wait for them to ferment for weeks on end. You need pickles *now.* You could try to find a time machine and travel to the future. Or try quick pickles—quickles! A snacky side with seriously low effort, these quickles are perhaps one of the most flexible recipes in this book. Use your favorite vegetable or fruit and any vinegar from your pantry to put your own spin on it.

½ pound **vegetable** or **fruit** (see Bee Flexible!)

2 tablespoons **vinegar**, such as rice vinegar, red wine vinegar, or sherry vinegar

Coarse salt

1. Carefully use a sharp knife or a vegetable slicer to thinly slice or dice the vegetable or fruit into bite-size pieces. (The smaller you cut the vegetable or fruit, the quicker it will pickle!)

2. In a small bowl, toss the cut vegetable or fruit with the vinegar. Season lightly with a sprinkle of salt and set aside for 10 minutes to lightly pickle. Enjoy!

Try different ingredients:

* Tender vegetables such as cucumbers, squash, and fresh corn
* Aromatic vegetables such as peeled and thinly sliced onions (red, yellow, or sweet), shallots, garlic, pearl onions, etc.
* Root vegetables that are edible when raw, such as radishes, beets, carrots, parsnips
* Fresh fruit such as berries, firm tomatoes, mangoes, papayas

Add a flavor boost:

* **OILS:** Add 1 tablespoon roasted peanut or toasted sesame oil.
* **SPICES:** Sprinkle in ground spices such as coriander, cumin, turmeric, chile flakes, or black pepper.
* **HERBS:** Once pickled, fold in chopped fresh herbs such as sliced scallions, parsley, cilantro, dill, mint.
* **SWEETNESS:** Sprinkle in 1 teaspoon sugar, honey, or maple syrup to add a hint of sweetness to any pickle.

SERVES 2

TIME: 15 minutes

kimchi grilled cheese

2 tablespoons **unsalted butter**, at room temperature

4 slices **thick-cut country bread**, about ½ inch thick

4 ounces **mild cheddar cheese**, cut into 8 slices

¼ cup chopped drained **kimchi**

1 **scallion**, thinly sliced

A CLASSIC GRILLED cheese sandwich is a dream combo of textures and flavors: crispy, crusty, soft, and chewy. This combination packs a nice pickle-y punch with kimchi, a delicious fermented cabbage that is a staple in Korean cuisine. For the cheese, a mild cheddar, Gruyère, or mozzarella will do wonders as a brilliant partner to balance the kimchi's tartness (see Bee Flexible for more ideas!). And the bread is a helpful partner, too. A substantial sourdough, focaccia, or country loaf soaks up these flavors while retaining the sandwich's buttery crunch and shape.

1. Warm up a heavy skillet over medium heat. Spread some soft butter over one side of each slice of bread. Place 2 slices of bread, butter-side down, in the skillet. Top each slice of bread with 2 slices of cheddar and cook until the cheese begins to soften and melt, about 5 minutes.

2. Top one slice of bread with half the kimchi and half the sliced scallions. Use a spatula to flip the other (untopped) slice cheese-side down over the kimchi slice. Press down on the sandwich to adhere the slices.

3. Reduce the heat to medium-low and continue to cook, flipping the sandwich until both sides are golden and crisp and the cheesy filling is melted, about 2 minutes.

4. Transfer the sandwich to a board and repeat to make a second sandwich.

BEE FLEXIBLE!

- You can use any semi-firm cheese you like, such as provolone, Monterey Jack, or mozzarella.
- Try substituting kimchi with other fermented or pickled vegetables, such as sauerkraut that you find on Reuben sandwiches or crisp sour pickles that are typically served on fried chicken sandwiches.

SERVES 6 to 8

TIME: 10 minutes, plus 4 hours freezing time

give-it-a-swirl semifreddo

1½ cups (9 ounces) **chopped mango** or **other fruit**, fresh or frozen

Grated **zest and juice of 1 lime**

6 tablespoons **sugar**

Coarse salt

1 cup canned **unsweetened coconut cream**

2 cups **whole-milk plain Greek yogurt**

1 teaspoon **vanilla extract**

½ cup **unsweetened coconut flakes**

DO ALL PICKLES have to be savory? Afraido not! *Semifreddo* means "half frozen" in Italian, and this dish makes for a versatile dessert that everyone will love. Coconut cream substitutes for the usual heavy cream and captures the richness of a classic semifreddo. Nearly all semifreddos are paired with a healthy dose of sweet, bright fruit or fruit puree. In this recipe, we're going to push the tartness and sweetness to the max by quickling the mango with lime juice. That way, the contrast between the coconut and the mango adds a thrill to every bite.

1. In a small bowl, combine the mango, lime zest, lime juice, 2 tablespoons of the sugar, and a pinch of salt. Toss the ingredients together, using a fork to lightly crush the fruit pieces as you stir. Cover and keep chilled.

2. In a large bowl with a handheld mixer, whip the coconut cream to soft peaks, about 2 minutes. Add the yogurt, vanilla, ½ teaspoon salt, and the remaining 4 tablespoons sugar and whisk until the mixture is light and fluffy, about 2 minutes.

3. Pour the coconut cream mixture into a 1¾- to 2-quart baking dish or pan. Swirl in the mango by using a fork to drag and fold it into the creamy base. Wrap the pan with plastic wrap and freeze for at least 4 hours and up to 12 hours.

4. In a small dry skillet, toast the coconut flakes over medium heat, stirring frequently and watching as the edges begin to brown. Remove from the heat as soon as the flakes turn golden brown, about 3 minutes.

5. Remove the semifreddo from the freezer about 10 minutes before serving. Slice or scoop it into bowls and top with the toasted coconut flakes.

BEE FLEXIBLE!

Try a different fruit for a different swirl on your semifreddo! Pineapple, papaya, apricots, plums, or any berry would all taste great with the creamy coconut.

RICE

MAKES 4½ cups

TIME: 30 minutes

simple fluffy rice

2 cups **Japanese short-grain rice**, rinsed and drained

½ teaspoon **salt**, plus more to taste

2 tablespoons **rice vinegar** (optional, but highly recommended)

SHORT-GRAIN RICE IS known for its wide, plump grains. When cooked, the rice becomes tender and sticky, clumping together easily. This makes it great for dishes where the cooked rice needs to be shaped, molded (such as sushi or Hands-On Onigiri, page 60), or kneaded into a dough like mochi.

But it's also great served fluffy under Omurice (page 72), in a rice bowl (see Glazy Mushrooms with Tofu, page 98), or alongside Salty's Roasted Fish (page 38).

1. In a medium pot, stir together the drained rice, salt, and 2¼ cups water. Bring to a boil over high heat, then reduce the heat to medium-low, cover (setting the lid slightly off to leave about a ¼-inch opening between the pot and the lid), and cook until the rice is softened and tender, about 15 minutes.

2. Remove from the heat and slide the lid to cover the pot tightly. Let sit for an additional 10 minutes.

3. Lift the lid, pour in the rice vinegar (if using), and season with additional salt. Fluff the grains and use as directed in a recipe or divide among bowls and serve.

MAKES 8 onigiri

TIME: 20 minutes, plus time for cooking the rice

hands-on onigiri

THIS RECIPE PUTS the chewy, doughy, and sticky qualities of cooked rice right into the palm of your hand. A stuffed rice treat, *onigiri* is comfort food that has a long history in Japanese cuisine. It can come in all kinds of cool shapes, including triangles, cylinders, and spheres, and be stuffed with whatever you're craving for lunch or a snack. You can add flavor and color to the cooked rice and the filling by mixing in soy sauce or a variety of condiments. You can even cut little eyes and mouths out of the nori, or seaweed, and place them on your rice creation to make *kyaraben*, which is *onigiri* decorated to look like your favorite friends, like Mochi! Ready to play with your food?

4 cups **Simple Fluffy Rice** (page 59)

½ cup **filling** (see The Rice Stuff)

8 pieces **nori**, cut into 3- to 4-inch squares, plus additional nori for making kyaraben

Sesame seeds, for garnish (optional)

1. Prepare a bowl of water for wetting your hands to keep the rice from sticking to your fingers while you work. When the rice is cool enough to handle, place ¼ cup of rice in your palm.

2. Using your thumb, form an indent in the rice, then place about 2 teaspoons of filling inside. Top with another ¼ cup rice. With moistened hands, form the rice into any shape you desire. Press and mold the rice to compact it around the filling.

3. Wrap the molded rice with a square of seaweed, pressing lightly to adhere it to your onigiri. If making kyaraben, use scissors to cut eyes and mouths out of the extra nori, then press the cutouts directly onto the molded rice (chopsticks can be helpful for placing the cutouts). Sprinkle the rice with sesame seeds (if using). Repeat to make 7 more. Serve.

THE RICE STUFF

You can stuff your *onigiri* with any filling of your choice. Try these traditional fillings to start. What fillings do you want to try?

- Chopped umeboshi (jarred pickled plums)
- Umami's Favorite Mushrooms (page 97)
- Katsuo (dried bonito flakes)
- Tuna mayo (combine 1 can of drained flaked tuna with 1 tablespoon Kewpie mayonnaise, which is a Japanese mayo packed with umami!)

MAKES one 9-inch cake

TIME: 90 minutes (includes time for cooling!)

mochi's spiced cake

¾ cup **unsalted butter**, plus more for the pan

½ teaspoon **ground cinnamon**

¼ teaspoon **ground nutmeg**

¼ teaspoon **ground allspice**

1¾ cups **glutinous sweet rice flour**

½ cup **unsweetened coconut flakes**

½ cup **light brown sugar**

¾ teaspoon **baking powder**

DID YOU KNOW **Waffles's best friend, Mochi, is made of rice? It's true! He was created with a special kind of short-grain rice called glutinous sweet rice. When cooked, the rice becomes very sticky and can be pounded into a paste and then formed into mochi, which is a special dessert traditionally served during the Japanese New Year. The rice can also be powdered into a flour that you can buy to make—that's right—mochi cake! This recipe is a tribute to Waffles's dearest friend, who, like this cake, is sweet and just spicy enough to keep things fun. Who is your best friend?**

1. Preheat the oven to 350°F. Generously butter a 9-inch round cake pan and line a small baking sheet with parchment paper.

2. Place the butter in a medium saucepan and set over medium heat. Cook, stirring with a wooden spoon or spatula until the butter foams and turns dark golden brown, 10 to 12 minutes. Remove from the heat, stir in the cinnamon, nutmeg, and allspice and allow to cool slightly. It should smell wonderfully fragrant and nutty!

3. In a small bowl, whisk together ½ cup of the rice flour, the coconut flakes, 2 tablespoons of the brown sugar, ¼ teaspoon of the baking powder, and ¼ teaspoon of the salt. Pour in ¼ cup of the brown butter and rub it into the dry ingredients with your fingers to form a loose crumb. Spread the crumb in an even layer on the lined baking sheet and toast in the oven until light golden brown, about 10 minutes.

4. In a large bowl, combine the coconut milk, the remaining 6 tablespoons brown sugar, the eggs, pumpkin, and vanilla. Whisk to incorporate.

(INGREDIENTS AND RECIPE CONTINUE)

¾ teaspoon **coarse salt**

1 cup **unsweetened coconut milk**

2 whole **eggs**, lightly beaten

¼ cup **pumpkin puree**

1 teaspoon **vanilla extract**

Store-bought caramel sauce or **chocolate sauce** (optional)

Whipped cream or **ice cream**, for serving

5. In a small bowl, combine the remaining 1¼ cups sweet rice flour, ½ teaspoon baking powder, and ½ teaspoon salt. Fold the dry mixture into the wet and combine until there are no dry pockets. Fold in the remaining ½ cup spiced brown butter. Pour the plain batter into the prepared cake pan.

6. Bake until the center of the cake is set and the top is a deep golden brown, 50 to 60 minutes. Transfer the cake to a wire rack and allow it to cool in the pan for at least 10 minutes. Run a knife around the sides of the cake pan to loosen and place a plate over the pan. Invert the cake onto the plate, then invert again onto the wire rack. Allow the cake to cool completely.

7. Once cooled, spread a thin, even layer of the caramel or chocolate syrup (if using) over the top of the cake. Line the edge of the cake with the golden brown crumble. Serve with soft whipped cream or ice cream.

RICE AROUND THE WORLD

Mochi learned that he has rice in his family tree. Most family trees show how people in a family are all connected. We often think of family as moms, dads, grandmas, and baby sisters. But family can be all the people you love—the people in your community, the friends you help, and the friends who help you. Family comes in all sizes, shapes, and colors—like rice.

Almost every part of the world has dishes made from rice. Rice can be red, black, brown, or white. Its grains can be long and pointy or short and stubby. Sometimes rice dishes are spicy, like *jambalaya* from New Orleans, and sometimes they can be sweet, like *rice pudding* from Sweden or Portugal. Sometimes they're crunchy, like *bibimbap* from South Korea, and sometimes they're creamy, like *risotto* from Italy. Indian *biryani* is savory and toasty, whereas Vietnamese *xôi ngũ sắc* is sticky and brightly colored. No matter what kind of rice you're making, you're part of the long, deep history that has brought this important ingredient to every corner of the world and back again many times over.

The truth is, we are all connected, especially when we learn, cook, and eat together!

Here is the world of rice. What rice dishes do you want to try?

- China: fried rice
- Hawaii: loco moco
- South Korea: bibimbap
- Venezuela: criollo
- India: biryani
- Ghana: jollof
- Denmark: risalamande
- New Orleans: jambalaya
- Vietnam: xôi ngũ sắc
- Colombia: coconut rice
- Uzbekistan: Uzbek plov
- England: kedgeree
- Portugal: arroz doce
- Sweden: rice pudding

EGG

SERVES 4

TIME: 5 to 15 minutes

the shape-shifter egg

4 large **eggs**

Salt and freshly cracked black pepper

AS AN INGREDIENT, eggs are the ultimate shape-shifters—an egg can morph from runny to jammy to hard-set, all with boiling water. The beauty of a boiled egg is in its simplicity. Peel off the shell, cut it open, and sprinkle it with salt for a quick protein snack. You can stir soft-boiled eggs into soups for a creamy finish or slice a hard-boiled egg over a grain salad—the possibilities are limitless! And what's more, cooked eggs can be made ahead of time and stored easily in the fridge.

1. Bring a medium pot of water to a gentle simmer over medium heat. You should see steam and medium-size bubbles rising to the surface of the water. Using a slotted spoon, gently lower the eggs into the pot one at a time.

2. How do you want your eggs? It's up to you! Check out the chart on pages 70 and 71 for cooking times, which range from 5 to 15 minutes. Don't forget to set your timer! Listen for it to chime, and once it does, use a slotted spoon to transfer the eggs to a bowl.

3. Run the eggs under cold tap water to stop the cooking process. Once cool, gently crack the shell on all sides by tapping the egg on a hard surface. Peel off the shell. For soft-boiled eggs, gently crack the eggshell, then use the tip of a spoon to peel the shell without breaking the yolk.

4. To serve a medium- or hard-boiled egg, break or slice the egg down the middle, then sprinkle each half with a little salt and pepper. To enjoy a soft-boiled egg, set the peeled egg in a bowl, sprinkle with salt and pepper, and break the yolk with a spoon. Now take a bite!

TEX'S EGG INDEX

HOW DO *YOU* LIKE YOUR EGGS?

Cookin' an egg changes its texture, which is all about how it feels on your tongue. So quit stallin' and start boilin' so you can find your favorite egg texture—or *teggsture*!

Soft-Boiled

TIME: 5 minutes

TEXTURE: Soft, runny, and jiggly all over like a jellyfish

ENJOY OVER: soup, ramen, pasta, porridge

Jammy

TIME: 7 minutes

TEXTURE: Solid egg white and semi-solid yolk—it stands on its own

ENJOY WITH: toast, grain salad bowls, or alone as a snack

Boiled

TIME: 9 minutes

TEXTURE: Set enough to slice—firm white and bright-yellow yolk

GREAT FOR: toast, salad, or pickling

Hard-Boiled

TIME: 11 to 15 minutes

TEXTURE: Firmly set—no ifs, ands, or buts about it

GREAT FOR: chopping into salad, crushing into dressings

Extra Egg

TIME: That's not an egg, that's Mochi!

TEXTURE: Don't cook Mochi!

GREAT FOR: Mochi is perfect just the way he is.

SERVES 1

TIME: 30 minutes (including time for the rice)

omurice

IN EPISODE 6, **Waffles and Mochi met Chef Motokichi Yukimura in Kyoto, Japan, who introduced them to *omurice*, a fluffy, custardy omelet that's served over rice. It's a simple egg dish that's a modern staple for many kids in Japan—and it's served with ketchup! If you don't quite get the texture or the look right the first—or the twelfth—time you make it, that's okay because it is still every bit as tasty. You can substitute the ketchup with your favorite sauce, such as oyster sauce or hot sauce.**

Plating *omurice* is almost as enjoyable as it is to dive into and might make you say *oishi*! That means "delicious" in Japanese. So are you ready to become the omelet master? Time to get cracking!

2 large **eggs**, lightly beaten

Coarse salt

1 cup **Simple Fluffy Rice** (page 59)

1 tablespoon **neutral oil**, such as grapeseed or canola

Ketchup, for serving

1. In a small bowl, beat the eggs with 1 teaspoon water. Season with a pinch of salt.

2. Make a rice mound by placing the rice on a plate and using your hands to shape it into a smooth, rounded heap.

3. In a nonstick medium skillet, heat the oil over low heat for about 30 seconds. Pour in the beaten eggs. Swirl the pan over the heat and stir the eggs repeatedly with chopsticks or a small spatula. As the eggs begin to curdle slightly, after about 30 seconds, allow them to cook undisturbed until the bottom sets and the surface looks custardy, about 30 seconds. Remove the pan from the heat so you don't overcook the egg. Run the chopsticks or small spatula around the edge of the omelet.

4. To fold, use the handle to lift and tilt the pan away from you at an angle. Lift the edge of the cooked egg closest to you and fold it into the middle to cover one-third of the omelet, then fold the whole omelet over again to roll up and cover the remaining edge. Keeping the pan tipped, cook the egg for another 10 seconds to seal the edge.

5. Serve immediately by sliding the omelet gently off the pan and right on top of the rice mound. Slice the omelet along the top to open up the custardy middle. Drizzle with some ketchup and dig in!

GOOD EGGFORT!

Folding the eggs will take some practice as they cook rather quickly even over low heat. If you find your eggs have lost their custardy texture while you are folding, that's okay. A firm-set omelet is still edible, so waste not! Enjoy the omelet over the rice mound with some ketchup and try again next time.

SERVES 4

TIME: 30 minutes

tortellini soup

8 cups **chicken** or **vegetable broth**

2 ounces **Parmigiano-Reggiano cheese rinds** (see Shhh . . . Here's a Cheffy Secret)

2 **garlic cloves**, smashed and peeled

1 **bay leaf**

6 to 8 **thyme sprigs**

Salt and freshly ground black pepper

1 pound **cheese tortellini**, store-bought, fresh or frozen

2 tablespoons chopped **fresh parsley**

¼ cup grated **parmesan cheese**

OUR FRIEND CHEF Massimo Bottura—one of the most famous chefs in the world—taught us in Italy how to make tortellini with flour and eggs. It was the dish that made Mochi realize he liked eggs!

There are so many delicious ways to enjoy this stuffed fresh pasta, but this soup-like dish is a delicious place to start. With a few simple ingredients and some store-bought tortellini, you can create a delicate, savory dish that you'll remember long after you've finished the last drop.

1. In a medium pot, combine the broth Parmigano rinds, garlic, bay leaf, and thyme. Bring the broth to a boil over high heat. Then reduce to a simmer and cook over medium-low heat until the liquid is reduced by one-quarter, about 25 minutes.

2. Strain out the solids using a slotted spoon or by pouring the liquid through a fine-mesh sieve into a bowl. Season the broth to taste with salt and pepper.

3. Bring the broth to a simmer over medium-high heat. Carefully add the tortellini to the broth a few at a time. Cook until all of the tortellini float to the surface of the liquid, about 5 minutes. Taste the broth for seasoning and add more salt if needed. Remove from the heat.

4. Divide the tortellini and broth among four bowls. Garnish each bowl with the parsley, grated parmesan, and additional pepper. Serve immediately.

Shhh . . .
Here's a Cheffy Secret

The next time you buy parmesan, get a wedge with a rind. You can grate the cheese yourself (#parmarm workout will make you strong!) and save the rinds for adding to soups or broths. If you don't have rinds, add more parmesan to taste.

MAKES 9 meringues

TIME: 1 hour 30 minutes

cloud meringues

THESE BAKED MERINGUES are like the clouds that Magicart flies through. They're light and simple and can be made using an electric mixer or the energetic enthusiasm of an eager collaborator—specifically, their arm! Whoever or whatever it takes to do the whipping, your egg whites will transform from liquid slime to billowy peaks to crispy treats. Every bite of this dessert is fun for all your taste buds—crunchy and smooth, tart and sweet!

4 large **egg whites**, at room temperature

¼ teaspoon **cream of tartar**

¼ cup **sugar**

¼ teaspoon **ground cardamom**

Pinch of **fine sea salt**

½ cup **pistachios**, very finely chopped (see Tasty Tip)

½ cup store-bought **lemon curd**

1 cup **fresh berries**, such as blueberries, cut strawberries, raspberries, or blackberries

¼ cup fresh **mint leaves**, for garnish

1. Preheat the oven to 275°F. Line a baking sheet with parchment paper and trace nine 3-inch circles using a pencil and a round biscuit cutter or the bottom of a bottle. Flip over the paper so the circles are on the bottom but you can still see them.

2. In the bowl of a stand mixer fitted with the whisk attachment (or in a large bowl with a handheld mixer), beat the egg whites at low speed until foamy. Gradually increase the speed and whip the egg whites until soft peaks begin to form, 2 to 3 minutes. Sprinkle in the cream of tartar and add the sugar 1 tablespoon at a time until all the sugar is incorporated. Add the cardamom and salt.

3. Turn the mixer speed to high and beat until the egg whites are glossy and stiff peaks form. Using a wooden spoon or spatula, gently work

Tasty Tip

You can chop the pistachios in a small food processor or you can do it by hand. Pour the pistachios into a sturdy plastic bag and lay it flat on the counter. Bang with a rolling pin or bottle until the nuts are broken up into small pieces.

half of the ground pistachios into the stiff whites, folding in just enough to streak the batter.

4. Transfer about three heaping spoonfuls of the meringue to each traced circle on the lined baking sheet. Flatten the tops just enough to spread the meringue to the edge of each circle.

5. Bake the meringues until dry and crisp, about 45 minutes. Turn off the oven and allow the meringue to cool in the oven for an additional 15 minutes. Transfer to a cooling rack and cool completely.

6. To serve, crack the top of each meringue using the back of a spoon and place it on a plate. Spoon in some lemon curd. Top each meringue with berries, the remaining chopped pistachios, and lots of fresh mint leaves for garnish.

HERBS
& SPICES

MAKES a heaping ½ cup

TIME: 10 minutes

better than butter

1 large **lemon**

2 sticks (8 ounces) **unsalted butter**, at room temperature

1 teaspoon **freshly ground black pepper**

2 tablespoons chopped **fresh basil**

1 tablespoon chopped **fresh parsley**

1½ teaspoons **fine sea salt**

2 teaspoons **honey** (optional), preferably buckwheat

ARE YOU READY to be a flavor explorer? This special butter will send you on an expedition to the bright peaks of lemon zest, the earthy valleys of black pepper, and the grassy fields of basil and parsley. But the secret ingredient is . . . heat! Herby and spiced butters like this one really come alive when they meet anything browned, baked, roasted, or steamed. Imagine a smear of this butter melting over a hot slice of toast, softening into the nooks and crannies of Herby Smashed Potatoes (page 44) or Umami's Favorite Mushrooms (page 97). Yum!

1. Grate the lemon zest by running the lemon skin against the holes of a Microplane or fine rasp-style grater. Rotate the lemon as you run it against the grater to make sure you are grating only the yellow portions of the skin where all the delicious, bright lemon oils live. The white part of the lemon is quite bitter, so you'll want to avoid grating that as you zest.

2. In a large bowl, combine the softened butter, lemon zest, pepper, basil, parsley, salt, and honey (if using). Stir with a rubber spatula to incorporate until the butter is creamy.

3. If using immediately, move the butter to a small bowl to use. If making ahead, transfer the butter to a sheet of plastic wrap or parchment paper and scrape together using the spatula. Roll the plastic or parchment over the butter and shape into a log. Roll the log on the work surface to make sure it is evenly shaped, then twist the ends of the wrap to secure. Store in the refrigerator for up to 1 week or store in the Land of Frozen Foods for up to 1 month.

SERVES 4

TIME: 10 minutes

pop à la corn

POPCORN MAY BE the perfect snack for movie night, but as a base for experimenting with flavors, it is a chef's dream! What starts as a hard, waxy corn seed becomes something airy and crispy with a little oil and lots of heat. Once you have popped all the kernels, you can work your cheffy magic with your favorite combination of flavorings.

With this recipe, cayenne and lime get even zingier when they meet the fresh, hot kernels, which will hold the flavor long after cooling, too. Ready to pop to it?

1 tablespoon grated **lime zest**

1¼ teaspoons **fine sea salt**

1 teaspoon **sugar**

½ teaspoon **cayenne pepper**

6 tablespoons **coconut oil** or a **neutral oil** such as canola

½ cup **popcorn kernels**

1. In a small bowl, combine the lime zest, salt, sugar, and cayenne. Set aside.

2. In a large Dutch oven or soup pot set over medium heat, pour in 4 tablespoons of the oil and the popcorn kernels. Stir to coat the kernels with oil. Once the oil starts to heat up, cover the pot with a tight-fitting lid.

3. Now, shhh . . . listen as the first kernels begin to pop. Can you hear them? After about a minute, pick up the pot and give it a good shake. This allows any unpopped kernels to sink to the bottom. You'll start to hear lots more popping noises and once the popping begins to slow down, turn off the heat and let the pot sit, covered, for another 30 seconds.

4. Remove the lid and transfer the popped corn to a large bowl.

5. Drizzle in the remaining 2 tablespoons of oil, sprinkle in your chile-lime mixture, and toss to coat evenly. Serve and enjoy!

BEE FLEXIBLE!

Substitute the chile-lime mix with any of the seasoned salts on pages 30 and 31.

MAKES about 2 cups

TIME: 45 minutes

crispy chickpeas

THIS IS AN easy snack that gives our star ingredient—the seasoning salts—a chance to show off. Cooked chickpeas are plump, juicy, creamy, and nutty. Roasting them until they're crispy deepens their earthy flavor. What they lose in juiciness they gain in texture: They become crunchy on the outside but chewy on the inside. They are also perfect partners for other tasty flavors. A sprinkle of salt would be fine, but toss in some Za'atar (page 31) and you now have a snack fit for the greatest chefs, or a savvy side for a lunch that needs a boost.

2 (15.5-ounce) cans **chickpeas**, drained and rinsed

¼ cup **olive oil**, plus more if needed

2 tablespoons **seasoning salt** (see pages 30 and 31)

1. Preheat the oven to 400°F.

2. Spread the chickpeas on a sheet pan and pat them very dry with paper towels or a thin kitchen towel. Drizzle them with the olive oil until they are coated in oil (use more if necessary).

3. Roast until they turn light golden brown and become crunchy, about 30 minutes. Shake the chickpeas on the pan at least once midway through the roasting process to stir and at the same time rotate the baking sheet front to back. Turn off the oven and allow the chickpeas to sit for another 10 minutes.

4. Remove the pan from the oven and sprinkle the still-hot chickpeas with the seasoning salt, stirring to make sure to coat every little pea.

5. Allow to cool slightly before serving. To store, let them completely cool and keep at room temperature in an airtight container for up to 1 week.

SERVES 6

TIME: 30 minutes

preeti's pani puri party

WHEN ALL THE herbs and spices disappeared from the grocery store, Waffles and Mochi quickly learned how important these two ingredients are. After all, as Waffles noted, a world without flavor has no life. No color. That's a world no one should have to live in!

To get Waffles and Mochi cooking with flavor, our chef friend Preeti Mistry introduced them to pani puri, a street food sold in roadside stalls in India. It's a great way to enjoy *chaat*, which are Indian snack foods that are often crunchy and savory, and always packed with flavor. These fried crisps are the right vehicle for a creamy potato and chickpea filling. They are fun to assemble with friends and toss onto your taste buds! But before you do, add a little tomato and fresh herbs. The puree of tamarind pods, which come from a tree, takes your taste buds on a wild, tangy ride with each bite.

Oil for frying

1 (7-ounce) package **pani puri coins**

2 **Yukon Gold potatoes**, peeled and cut into 1-inch pieces

Coarse salt

1 (15.5-ounce) can **chickpeas**, drained and rinsed

2 tablespoons **tamarind puree**

½ cup small firm **cherry tomatoes**, halved or quartered if large

¼ cup minced **red onion**

¼ cup **fresh basil leaves**, chiffonade (see Tasty Tip)

¼ cup **fresh cilantro**, chopped

1. Set up a wire rack in a sheet pan or line a baking sheet or large plate with paper towels.

2. In a large, deep saucepan, pour in 2 inches of the oil and heat over medium heat. After 10 minutes, add one puri coin to test the oil; if it puffs up, your oil is ready! Fry the rest of the puri coins until they are puffed up and light golden brown, about 30 seconds each. Be careful not to crowd the pan since they will grow. Drain on the rack or paper towels.

3. In a small pot, combine the potatoes with water to cover and season with salt. Bring to a boil over medium-high heat. Then reduce the heat to a simmer and cook until the potatoes are cooked through and tender, about 12 minutes. Drain off any liquid (leaving the potatoes in the pot), add the canned chickpeas, and lightly crush everything together with a fork. Taste and add more salt if necessary.

4. In a small bowl, combine the tamarind puree with ¼ cup water.

Tasty Tip

Chiffonade may sound like a hairdo, but it's a cooking technique! To chiffonade herbs, stack them up and roll them as you would a sleeping bag. Then use your trusty scissors to snip the roll into long strips.

5. To assemble, punch a hole in the top of each pani puri with a teaspoon. Fill the inside of each with the potato and chickpea mixture. Top each with tomato and onions. Pour in about 1 teaspoon of the tamarind water and sprinkle with basil and cilantro. Pop a whole pani puri in your mouth to kick off the party!

CORN

SERVES 4

TIME: 15 minutes

simple buttery corn

Coarse salt

4 ears **corn**, husked

2 tablespoons **unsalted butter** or **Better Than Butter** (page 79), at room temperature

Sea salt (optional), for sprinkling

PERHAPS THE BEST way to really enjoy corn is when it's freshest. A lightly boiled or grilled ear of corn reveals the sweet and milky character of the perfectly plump kernels. This recipe keeps it simple, with a generous dab of soft butter and a sprinkle of sea salt. You can also put to use a pat of Better Than Butter (page 79) for an herby finish, or check out the tips for more ideas.

1. Bring a large pot of salted water to a boil over medium-high heat. Using tongs, carefully drop the ears of corn into the pot and allow them to cook for 10 minutes.

2. Remove the pot from the heat and use tongs to transfer the cooked corn to a platter.

3. Add wooden skewers to the ends of each cob to make handles. Slather each ear of corn with softened butter and sprinkle with several pinches of sea salt (if using) to enjoy. (If using the Better Than Butter, which already has salt in it, taste the corn before sprinkling on additional salt.)

SERVES 4

TIME: 30 minutes

creamy grits with jammy eggs

CORN IS DELICIOUS fresh, but it's also great to eat once it's dried and then boiled in water. Chef Mashama Bailey taught Waffles and Mochi how to make grits, which is dried and ground-up corn. She loves cooking it because it helps her learn about her ancestors. By eating what they ate, she feels connected to them. How cool is that!

Grits are one of the many corn porridges that can be found in cuisines across the globe. Mămăligă in Romania, pashofa in the Chickasaw Nation of America, and polenta in Italy are just a few examples. What makes all these dishes so wonderful is how well they work as a base—a part of a dish that serves as the foundation for other flavors. Here, you'll be cheesing up your creamy cornmeal (see Bee Flexible for ideas). Then top your bowl of grits with a soft-boiled egg for a simple yet nourishing meal.

1 cup **white** or **yellow grits**

Coarse salt

3 ounces **sharp cheddar cheese**, grated

Freshly ground black pepper

2 tablespoons **unsalted butter**

4 **soft-boiled eggs** (see page 70)

1. In a medium saucepan, heat 3 cups water over medium heat. Whisk in the grits and season lightly with salt. Reduce the heat and cook at a simmer, stirring occasionally, until the grits are tender, 20 to 25 minutes.

2. Whisk in the cheddar and stir until it melts into the grits. Taste the grits. Do they need more seasoning? If so, add a pinch of salt and some pepper. Stir in the butter until melted.

3. Divide the grits among four bowls. Peel the boiled eggs, slice each egg down the middle, and set on top of the grits. Serve warm.

BEE FLEXIBLE!

- For extra-creamy grits, substitute 1 cup milk for 1 cup of the water and cook as directed.
- Don't have sharp cheddar cheese? No problem! Use any hard cheese such as parmesan, Pecorino Romano, Gruyère, Asiago, Comté, or Emmental.

SERVES 6 to 8

TIME: 40 minutes

corntest-winning corn bread

WHEN WAFFLES AND Mochi lost all their corn and Cheryl burned her corn bread during the Corn Cooking Contest, instead of giving up, Waffles suggested they all be flexible and work together to make some delicious corn bread. They joined forces and won the competition together!

Likewise, making this recipe is better with besties, family, or anyone else who wants to lend a hand. It's a team effort, and that goes for what's in the pan, too. Buttermilk and honey work brilliantly together to add richness and a light sweetness. This recipe is so easy—you'll want to share it with your family, friends, and neighbors!

1 stick (4 ounces) **unsalted butter**, melted, plus more for greasing the pan

1½ cups finely ground **yellow cornmeal**

¾ cup **all-purpose flour**

3½ teaspoons **baking powder**

¼ teaspoon **baking soda**

1 teaspoon **salt**

2 cups **full-fat buttermilk**

¼ cup **honey**

2 large **eggs**

Better Than Butter (page 79), for serving

1. Preheat the oven to 400°F. Grease a 9 × 9-inch baking pan or 9-inch ovenproof skillet.

2. In a medium bowl, whisk together the cornmeal, flour, baking powder, baking soda, and salt. Use your fingers to dig a well in the center of the dry ingredients.

3. In a medium bowl or liquid measuring cup, combine the buttermilk, honey (if using), and eggs. Whisk just until the ingredients are incorporated.

4. Pour the buttermilk mixture into the well in the flour mixture and use a wooden spoon or a spatula to stir to combine. Fold in the melted butter. Pour the batter into the baking pan and place it in the oven.

5. Bake until the top is lightly browned and the sides cleanly pull away from the pan, 25 to 30 minutes. Allow the corn bread to cool slightly before cutting into it.

6. Serve warm or at room temperature, spread with some Better Than Butter. Now that's what we call teamwork!

BEE FLEXIBLE!

Make this corn bread your very own with these ideas:

- **FOR CORNIER BREAD:** Add 1 cup of fresh or frozen sweet corn kernels to the batter for some texture and additional flavor.
- **FOR SPICIER BREAD:** Add some chopped chiles like jalapeños or serranos to the batter before baking.
- **FOR JAZZIER BREAD:** Amp up the flavor with some fresh herbs—chives or scallions work great here and will add a pop of color!
- **FOR MUFFINS:** Grease a 12-cup muffin tin and scoop the batter into the cups to make individual muffins. Bake at 350°F until a toothpick inserted in the center of a muffin comes out clean, 15 to 18 minutes, rotating the pan front to back halfway through the bake time.

SERVES 8

TIME: 20 minutes

champurrado

MAGICART TAUGHT WAFFLES and Mochi that corn can be a lot of stuff. In this chapter you've learned how to make corn on the cob, corn bread, and popcorn, but corn can also be turned into cornflakes, tamales, succotash, banku . . . and it can even make a delicious wintry drink. Let's learn how!

Champurrado is made from masa harina, which is a finely ground corn flour. The addition of chocolate, as well as spices and a pinch of salt, makes this a perfect warm drink to sip when it's cold outside or as an energizing breakfast to start your day. The key to this recipe is the whisking—you have to add the water slowly into the masa as you mix to keep it from clumping. Grab your favorite mug and let's get whisked away!

1 cup **masa harina**

4 ounces **Mexican chocolate** or **dark chocolate**, chopped

1 teaspoon **ground cinnamon**

¼ teaspoon **cayenne pepper**

½ teaspoon **salt**

½ cup chopped **piloncillo** or ¼ cup packed **dark brown sugar**

½ cup **milk**, **cream**, or **nut milk** of choice

1. Place the masa in a saucepan. In a slow, steady stream, whisk in 6 cups water while whisking constantly.

2. Set the pan over medium heat and bring to a gentle simmer, then cook, while whisking frequently, until the mixture thickens, about 15 minutes.

3. Reduce the heat to low and stir in the chocolate, cinnamon, cayenne, salt, and sugar. Stir until the chocolate is melted and the sugar dissolves. Whisk in the milk, then remove from the heat and serve immediately.

MEET MARVELOUS MASA!

Corn is what gives us masa, which is a light flour used to make tortillas, tamales, tacos, *tetelas*, *tlayudas*, and tostadas—which is why it is sometimes jokingly referred to as *vitamina T*, or vitamin T. Have you had your vitamin T today?

MUSHROOM

MAKES 3 cups

TIME: 15 minutes

umami's favorite mushrooms

THIS RICH TOPPING is almost as elegant as our taste bud Umami herself. She LOVES these mushrooms on toast, on pasta, with soft-boiled eggs, or on a bowl of corn grits! You'll need patience for this one to reveal its true power: Mushrooms take their time to release moisture and deepen in flavor.

This recipe uses Better Than Butter (page 79) and lots of different kinds of mushrooms. You may not recognize them at first, but that's okay! Give mushrooms a try and you might find that you love the delicious aromas filling your kitchen.

2 tablespoons **olive oil**, plus more as needed

1 pound **mixed mushrooms**, cleaned and halved or quartered if large

5 **garlic cloves**, smashed and peeled

4 **thyme sprigs**

Salt and freshly ground black pepper

2 tablespoons **Better Than Butter** (page 79), at room temperature

¼ cup chopped **fresh herbs**, for garnish

1. In a large skillet, heat the oil over medium heat. Working in batches so you don't crowd the skillet (and adding more oil as needed for each batch), add the mushrooms, garlic, and thyme. Cook, stirring frequently until the garlic begins to brown along the edges and the mushrooms are golden and tender, 10 to 12 minutes. Some mushrooms, like chanterelles, need the shorter amount of time, whereas sturdier mushrooms like cremini will benefit from a good long sauté.

2. Season to taste with salt and pepper. Add the butter and allow it to melt, stirring to coat the mushrooms in an even layer. Remove from the heat, discard the thyme stems, and toss in the fresh herbs. Serve.

SERVES 4

TIME: 25 minutes, plus time to make the sauce and rice

glazy mushrooms with tofu

1 (14-ounce) package **extra-firm tofu**, drained

1 pound **mixed mushrooms** (such as cremini, oyster, shiitake, and maitake), cleaned

1 cup **Salty-Sweet Sauce** (opposite)

3 tablespoons **olive oil**

¼ cup chopped **fresh herbs**, such as cilantro, basil, or parsley

4 cups **baby spinach** or any **baby leafy greens**

4 cups **Simple Fluffy Rice** (page 59)

SLOW-ROASTING MUSHROOMS IS a great way of achieving umami, but this recipe allows you to experience layer upon layer of umami! You'll achieve that through the glaze, a mix of miso paste and rice vinegar that melds effortlessly with the mushrooms as they bake on a sheet pan. And just what ingredient benefits from all this melding? Tofu, of course! Firm tofu slices are mighty lucky to share a pan with this mixture. The results, which you can serve alongside rice (and greens, too!), are like a master class in the way umami travels from one component of a dish to another.

1. Position two oven racks, one in the center and one in the top slot of the oven, and preheat the oven to 400°F.

2. Cut the block of tofu crosswise into four 1-inch-thick slices. Place the tofu slices on several sheets of paper towel to drain off the excess liquid. Tear or cut the mushrooms into 2-inch pieces.

3. Arrange the tofu evenly spaced and in a single layer on a sheet pan. Place the mushrooms between the tofu slices on the pan. Pour the sauce over the tofu and mushrooms, tossing with your hands to coat. Drizzle everything with the olive oil.

4. Transfer the pan to the center rack and roast the tofu and mushrooms until the glaze is set and begins to brown in spots on the tofu, about 20 minutes. Move the baking sheet to the upper rack and turn the broiler to high. Broil until the glaze is set and slightly charred in spots, about 5 minutes. Remove from the oven and scatter the fresh herbs over the top.

5. Divide the spinach and rice among four bowls. Top with the glazed mushrooms and tofu and serve immediately.

MAKES 1 cup **TIME:** 5 minutes

Salty-Sweet Sauce

6 tablespoons **soy sauce** or **tamari**

¼ cup **rice vinegar**

2 tablespoons **red miso**

1-inch piece **fresh ginger**, grated

1 **garlic clove**, grated

2 tablespoons **honey**

2 tablespoons **grapeseed oil**

1 teaspoon **toasted sesame oil** or **roasted peanut oil** (optional)

In a large bowl, whisk together the soy sauce, vinegar, miso, ginger, garlic, honey, grapeseed oil, and sesame oil (if using).

SERVES 6 to 8

TIME: 35 minutes

meaty mushroom quesadillas

4 tablespoons **neutral oil**, such as grapeseed or canola, plus more for the tortillas

1 pound **mixed mushrooms** (such as cremini, oyster, shiitake, and maitake), cleaned and halved or quartered if large

4 **garlic cloves**, sliced

2 teaspoons **cumin seeds** or 1 teaspoon **ground cumin**

Coarse salt and freshly ground black pepper

¼ cup **fresh cilantro**

8 large (8-inch) **flour** or **corn tortillas**

8 ounces **Oaxaca**, **Monterey Jack**, or **mozzarella cheese**, grated

Guacamole, **sour cream**, **and salsa**, for serving

A QUESADILLA CAN hold a variety of flavor combinations. The only required ingredient is the tortilla that encloses the ingredients. These mushroom quesadillas let the fungi shine. Any variety of mushrooms will do, but make sure to caramelize them over high heat (we're going for peak umami here!). A Oaxacan cheese provides some stretchy fun in each slice.

1. In a large skillet, heat 2 tablespoons of the oil over medium-high heat. Add half the mushrooms and cook without stirring until they begin to brown, about 5 minutes.

2. Add half the garlic and season the mushroom mixture with 1 teaspoon of the cumin seeds (or ½ teaspoon ground cumin) and salt and pepper to taste. Reduce the heat to medium and cook, stirring until any liquid evaporates and the cumin gets toasted and fragrant, about 2 minutes. Stir in half of the chopped cilantro. Move to a plate to cool.

3. Repeat with the remaining oil, mushrooms, garlic, cumin, and cilantro. Season with salt and pepper to taste and add to the plate.

4. Rinse and wipe out the skillet. Set the skillet over medium heat and drizzle in about 1 tablespoon of oil. Place a tortilla in the pan. Sprinkle some grated cheese over the tortilla, spread about 1½ tablespoons of the mushroom mixture over half of the tortilla, and heat for 1 minute. Fold the tortilla in half and cook for 2 minutes, pressing to adhere the sides.

5. Flip the quesadilla and cook until golden brown and the cheese is melted, about 1 minute. Remove to a plate and cover to keep warm. Repeat to make 7 more quesadillas. Cut into wedges and serve with guacamole, sour cream, and salsa.

WATER

WATER

The Most Important Ingredient

WATER IS A natural resource we use for washing our hands and hydrating our bodies, but did you know that it's also an essential ingredient in cooking? It might be the most important ingredient in the world! It's how we extract flavor from other ingredients, and it gives us a means of heating and cooling them. Let's investigate how to cook with water!

WHAT IS BLANCHING?

Blanching starts with boiling salted water and ends with an ice-cold bath to stop the cooking. It helps vegetables retain their bright color and prevents them from going limp. Chefs blanch herbs, snap peas, asparagus, and broccoli rabe.

WHAT IS STEAMING?

Steaming is cooking with water vapor. It's like boiling water, but ingredients sit in a basket above the water so the steam can cook the food. A lid keeps most of the steam from escaping. Steaming makes raw vegetables more easily digestible and more flavorful: Obviously we love the crunch of raw carrots, but steaming them can soften the crunch without affecting their flavor.

WHAT IS BOILING?

Boiling is for our hardiest and sturdiest ingredients. Each ingredient gives up some flavor to the water as it is boiled in a pot of water. Starches such as rice and grains, tubers such as potatoes and sweet potatoes, and legumes such as lentils and beans are all perfectly suited to being submerged in water and given a long, piping-hot bubble bath. With starches, grains, and legumes, start with cold water and bring it to a boil. For fresh vegetables like greens and corn, it is usually best to start with boiling water so the vegetables cook more evenly and more quickly.

MAKES 6 to 10 paletas

TIME: 5 minutes plus a minimum of 5 hours freezing time

freezie day paletas

3 cups **unsweetened rice milk**, store-bought or homemade (see Shhh . . . Here's a Cheffy Secret)

1 cup canned **unsweetened coconut cream**

1 tablespoon **ground cinnamon**, plus more for sprinkling

¼ teaspoon **ground nutmeg**

⅓ cup **sugar**

½ teaspoon **fine sea salt**

2 tablespoons **Sugar Spiced Salt** (optional; page 31)

WHEN WINTER ROLLS around, people celebrate all kinds of holidays, with lots of delicious foods! In Waffles and Mochi's home of the Land of Frozen Food, Freezie Day is the wow-iest time of the year, celebrated with a sweet frozen shaved ice. These paletas, or Popsicles, are easy to make at home—instead of shaving the ice, use Popsicle molds or paper cups. And they're delicious any time of year! No matter what traditions you celebrate, the best ones are always about being together. So be sure to share this treat with someone you love.

1. In a large pitcher or bowl, whisk together the rice milk, coconut cream, cinnamon, nutmeg, sugar, and salt until the sugar and salt are dissolved. Pour the mixture into ice pop molds or paper cups (which you will later fit with wooden pop sticks).

2. Freeze for 1 hour and insert the wooden sticks into the mixture. Continue to freeze until completely solid, 4 to 6 hours.

3. Pop the paletas out of the molds. If desired, roll in the sugar spiced salt. Serve immediately.

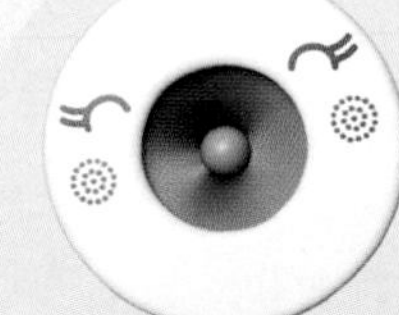

Shhh . . . Here's a Cheffy Secret

To make homemade rice milk, place 1 cup uncooked long-grain white rice in a bowl of water and cover with 2½ cups water. Soak for at least 4 hours and up to 8 hours. Pour the rice and soaking liquid into a blender and blend until all the rice is finely ground, 2 to 3 minutes. This recipe makes 3 cups.

SERVES 6 to 8

TIME: 50 minutes to 1 hour

chicken sancocho

WHETHER YOU'RE SITTING down to a rich bowl of *sancocho* in Panama, Ecuador, Colombia, Puerto Rico, or the Dominican Republic—to name just a few of the places you might find this dish—it brings together all the things we love about stew. You've got great roots and starches—like potato, yuca, and plantain. You've got a base seasoning that is wildly delicious—sofrito, which is a mix of peppers, onions, garlic, and culantro. And you've got a satisfying gravy-like broth—the result of the vegetables, seasoning, and stock lending their flavors to the water. This recipe, based on one by our friend Chef José Andrés, uses chicken as its protein, but there's room for smoked ham, pork, or beef; or the stew can be made vegetarian as well. The main theme of any great *sancocho* is that you can use what you have on hand to make it taste like home.

2 tablespoons **olive oil**

1 pound **bone-in, skin-on chicken parts**

Coarse salt

1 small **onion**, chopped

2 cups **Sofrito** (recipe follows)

½ teaspoon **achiote seeds**

1 bunch **scallions**, cut into 2-inch lengths

1 bunch **culantro**, torn into 2-inch strips (3 loose cups)

1 **medium yuca root**, peeled and cut into 1½-inch pieces

1 **green plantain**, peeled and cut into 1½-inch pieces

1 ear **yellow or white corn**, husked and cut crosswise into 2-inch pieces

1. Heat the oil in a large soup pot over medium heat. Season the chicken pieces with salt and place them skin-side down in the pan. Cook the chicken in batches, browning both sides, about 8 minutes per batch. Move the chicken to a plate.

2. Add the onion to the pan and sauté until softened, about 2 minutes. Stir in the sofrito and cook, scraping any browned bits on the bottom of the pot, until the liquid evaporates, about 3 minutes. Stir in the achiote, scallions, and culantro.

3. Add the yuca, plantain, and corn. Return the chicken pieces to the pot, nestling them among the vegetables. Season the chicken and vegetables with about 1 tablespoon coarse salt. Pour in 8 cups water, stir, and bring to a boil. Reduce the heat to a simmer and cook, uncovered, stirring occasionally until the chicken is tender and the vegetables begin to fall apart, about 15 minutes.

4. Taste and adjust the seasoning with more salt if necessary. Serve warm.

MAKES 4 cups **TIME:** 5 minutes

Sofrito

1 medium **red bell pepper**, cut into large chunks

4 **ají dulce** or **mini bell peppers**, halved

1 small **yellow onion**, chopped

2 large **plum tomatoes**, halved

4 **garlic cloves**, peeled

½ cup torn **fresh culantro leaves** (about 4 leaves) or 1 cup **culantro leaves and tender stems**

In a food processor or blender, combine the bell pepper, ají dulce, onion, tomatoes, and garlic and process to a coarse puree. Add the culantro and blend until smooth. Store in an airtight container in the refrigerator for up to 3 days or the freezer for up to 1 month.

SERVES 4 to 6

TIME: 50 minutes

gratitouille

ANY DISH WITH this many ingredients should be considered a celebration. We're really bringing out all the pantry has to offer so none of the flavors need to miss the party. This richly textured stew is your chance to take everything you've learned from this book about cooking and bring all of the ingredients together. Call this your grand finale! You'll taste rice, corn, potatoes, tomatoes, mushrooms, salt, spices and herbs, pickles, egg, and water in one showstopping dish. Make it to show gratitude to your friends and family for loving you for who you are. At the end of the meal, you can take in compliments to the chef—that's you!

¼ cup **olive oil**, plus more for serving

1 medium **white** or **yellow onion**, chopped

8 ounces **mushrooms**, such as cremini or shiitake

2 **garlic cloves**, minced or put through a garlic press

1 teaspoon **cumin seeds**

1 (14.5-ounce) can peeled **whole tomatoes**, undrained

1 **bay leaf**

2 **oregano** or **marjoram sprigs**

1 teaspoon **red pepper flakes**

Coarse salt

½ small **red onion** or 2 **shallots**, peeled and thinly sliced

2 tablespoons fresh **lime juice**

1. In a large Dutch oven, heat the oil over medium-high heat until shimmering, about 2 minutes. Add the chopped white onion and the mushrooms and cook, stirring frequently, until softened, about 6 minutes. Add the garlic and cumin seeds and cook until fragrant, about 2 minutes.

2. Slowly pour in the tomatoes and their juices, tearing the whole tomatoes into large chunks with your hands as you add them. Pop in the bay leaf, oregano, and pepper flakes, then stir. Pour in 4 cups water, stir, and bring the sauce to a boil. Reduce the heat and simmer until the liquid is slightly reduced and the sauce is just beginning to thicken, about 15 minutes. Season with salt.

3. Meanwhile, in a shallow bowl, combine the sliced red onions and lime juice. Season with a pinch of salt. Allow the onions to quick pickle while you finish the stew.

4. Carefully drop the potatoes into the pot, stir, and cook the stew until the potatoes are tender but not falling apart, about 14 minutes.

8 ounces **potatoes** (about 3 medium), such as Yukon Gold, scrubbed and halved or quartered if large

2 cups **corn kernels**, fresh or frozen

Simple Fluffy Rice (page 59), for serving

Soft-boiled egg (see page 70), for serving

1 cup mixed **fresh herbs**, such as dill or parsley

5. Stir in the corn and cook until warmed through, another 2 to 3 minutes. Taste the stew and adjust the seasoning by adding more salt if necessary.

6. To serve, divide the stew among shallow bowls. Top with some cooked rice, a soft-boiled egg, pickled red onions, and a handful of fresh herbs. Drizzle with some olive oil. Serve warm.

TRY IT!

SILLY CONVERSATION STARTERS

The best thing about eating is the food you get to taste! The second-best thing is spending time with the people who join you. There's nothing like a lively discussion around the dinner table. Try asking one another these questions the next time you share a meal.

What food would you fill a swimming pool with? Would you eat it or swim in it?

From Earth to Mars! How far would you fly for your favorite dish?

What's your favorite dance jam and what flavor of jam would you make to it?

If you could create any cereal flavor, what would it be? Chocolate cake crispies? Caramel banana Os? Roasted Brussels Sprout Crunch?

Which is your favorite meal of the day: breakfast, lunch, dinner, or when someone spills something on the floor (5-second rule counts!)?

Would you rather BE a helpful honeybee or a hungry ladybug in Mrs. O's garden?

Published in the United States by Clarkson Potter/Publishers, an imprint of Random House, a division of Penguin Random House LLC, New York.
clarksonpotter.com

CLARKSON POTTER is a trademark and POTTER with colophon is a registered trademark of Penguin Random House LLC.

Library of Congress Cataloging-in-Publication Data
Names: Komolafe, Yewande, author. | Marshall, Kelly, (Photographer) photographer. Title: Waffles + Mochi: based on the Netflix original series Waffles + Mochi, created by Erika Thormahlen and Jeremy Konner, featuring Michelle Obama / recipes by Yewande Komolafe ; photographs by Kelly Marshall. Description: New York: Clarkson Potter, 2021. | Audience: Ages 5–9 | Identifiers: LCCN 2021018913 (print) | LCCN 2021018914 (ebook) | ISBN 9780593234099 (hardcover) | ISBN 9780593234105 (ebook) Subjects: LCSH: Pancakes, waffles, etc. | LCGFT: Cookbooks.
Classification: LCC TX770 .W29 2021 (print) | LCC TX770 (ebook) | DDC 641.81/53—dc23
LC record available at https://lccn.loc.gov/2021018913
LC ebook record available at https://lccn.loc.gov/2021018914

ISBN 978-0-593-23409-9
Ebook ISBN 978-0-593-23410-5

Printed in Italy

Food Photographer: Kelly Marshall
Recipes: Yewande Komolafe
Sidebars: Christy Webster
Editor: Angelin Borsics
Designer: Jen Wang
Food & Prop Styling: Jillian Knox, assisted by Malina Syvoravong and Melina Kemph
Production Editor: Patricia Shaw
Production Manager: Kim Tyner
Composition: Merri Ann Morrell, Hannah Hunt, and Zoe Tokushige
Copy Editor: Kate Slate

10 9 8 7 6 5 4 3 2 1

First Edition